Academic Vocabulary with SPEED™:

Fostering Academic Vocabulary Mastery for English Learners and Struggling Students

Alexandra S. Guilamo

TaJu Educational Solutions, LLC

2958 North Nora

Chicago, IL 60634

www.tajulearning.com

2016 © TaJu Educational Solutions, LLC

All rights reserved. Expect permitted under the U.S. Copyright Act of 1976, no part of this book may be reproduced, distributed, or transmitted in any form or by any means, including by any electronic or mechanical means, including information storage and retrieval systems, without permission in writing by the author, except by a reviewer who may quote brief passages in a review.

SPEED Vocabulary™ is a registered Trademark of TaJu Educational Solutions, LLC

Printed in the United States of America.

DEDICATION

This book is dedicated to the students and educators who helped me to find my voice. Thank you for your willingness to be passionate learners.

CONTENTS

Introduction ii

Part 1 – A Foundation in Academic Vocabulary

1. How to Use This Book .... Pg 1
2. An Integrated Approach .... Pg 6
3. The 5 Elements of Vocabulary Instruction for ELLs and Struggling Learners .... Pg 15

Part 2 - Academic Vocabulary with SPEED™ in Action

4. Selecting "Just Right" Vocabulary to Acquire .... Pg 44
5. SPEED™ Vocabulary Weekly Lessons .... Pg 57

Appendix – Rolling Out SPEED™ Vocabulary

I. The First 45 Days .... Pg 88
II. Bibliography .... Pg 101

ACKNOWLEDGMENTS

I'd like to thank all the students who served as the inspiration to these lessons and all the teachers who've helped to refine each of these strategies. Many thanks to my family who supported me even when this book consumed me.

Introduction

When I was a teacher, I spent many hours planning ways to help my English language learners and struggling students to master the content. I differentiated. I scaffolded. I developed engaging and interrelated units full of games and novel activities. They still struggled in their own ways. One of many challenges was the fact that I had Mirella on one side of the room unable to comprehend the words of the content books that I was mandated to teach, and I had Kris on the other side of the room reading three levels beyond his grade.

At the end of the week, I remember the sheer exhaustion of looking at the impact of my teaching, the amount of energy I had poured into doing what it was that I loved most, and knowing that is was not enough. It was as though I had been trying to treat a broken arm with a Band-Aid. But if the solution wasn't the things I had been doing, then what was it?

I went through the stages of denial, first thinking that it was impossible for my students to achieve at the same levels as other students because, after all, they had just arrived in the United States, they were just learning English, or they had struggled in their educational path for years. I then left the land of denial and visited frustration for a while. After all, how could my sweet Mirella get to middle school barely knowing how to read? How could it be that she struggled so intensely with the ability to hold even a basic academic conversation? Soon after, I decided to wet off from the world of frustration, in order to begin working on a solution. The challenges that I was seeing made me think about the source or essential cause of the struggle she and many other students that I had seen over the years had. She was able to decode, she had phonemic awareness, and had built an impressive list of sight words that had helped her to grow in her reading level. But when it came down to it, there were just so many words that she did not know. This made comprehension of any text (chapter books, Science texts, Math books, and library books) something that left her overwhelmed and unsure of whether it was even worth it to try.

Years later, after becoming a principal, working at the district level to lead some of Chicago's most challenging schools, and moving back to coaching teachers, part of the solution became much more clear. When working with ELLs and struggling students, the range of needs is immense and intensely complicated. But I realized that the one common factor in schools that successfully supported ELLs and struggling students was their approach to language and vocabulary development. Did students have the vocabulary to learn content, to understand the books in front of them, and to discuss what it was that they were learning? This vocabulary "problem" was one that impacted my own classroom, and the hundreds of classrooms that I visited regardless of age, grade, gender, subject, language proficiency, or years of exposure to English.

It should not have been such a surprise to me. After all, I know that challenges with vocabulary strongly influence the readability of a text (Chall & Dale, 1995). Not only that, but lacking vocabulary is known to be a critical factor in overall school failure or success in disadvantaged students (Biemiller, 1999). Yes, it is a disheartening fact that ELLs and struggling students have notably lower vocabularies than their counterparts (Oller & Eilers, 2002), because these vocabularies are such strong predictors of overall achievement.

Not only that, but proficient, native English learners

acquire an estimated 3,000 new words each year in school (Nagy & Anderson, 1984). This vast number of words helps native English students achieve growth in reading comprehension and their ability to communicate mastery across content areas. The self-fulfilling prophecy is that this reading growth and content mastery creates the path for native speakers and students to, in turn, learn more words which will fuel even further growth down the line. But for EL's and struggling students, the challenge with vocabulary is greater than just acquiring the same 3,000 new words each year. These students come with such a range of size in their vocabulary (Snow & Kim, 2007), that it is almost impossible to calculate what it would take for these students to reach the same vocabularies, and by extension the same opportunity for school success, as their native classmates. It is because of this that it becomes almost impossible to have a singular approach to helping them catch up to their peers.

So what is the solution? Well, the solution needed to be one that blossomed from the uniqueness of each learner's situation and the reality of the schools in which they learn. The solution to this challenge came organically, from studying tons of research, watching great teachers, and analyzing the impact of different approaches on student learning and engagement. I call it SPEED™. SPEED™ stands for Say, Picture, Explain, Engage, and Discuss. This comprehensive vocabulary acquisition process that allows the interweaving of anchoring, background knowledge, explicit teaching, meaningful and varied practice, and metacognitive dialogue allows EL's and struggling students to acquire vocabulary words quickly and profoundly.

Since many studies suggest that the amount of instructional time devoted to building vocabulary is simply not enough, part of the SPEED™ approach includes teachers' willingness to commit to increase the amount of consideration given to vocabulary instruction. Again, the commitment is to consider vocabulary needs when planning, not to necessarily increase the amount of time. In parts 1 and 2 of this book, we will share simple and time-efficient ways of doing this. An additional piece that makes SPEED™ effective is that students are asked to develop goals around their word usage outside of vocabulary "time." This goal setting helps students transfer the knowledge of the vocabulary gained during safe practice into other situations and times when the term would be appropriate.

Finally, SPEED is effective because it is meant to be integrated into your current teaching approach and reality. For reading teachers who use balanced literacy, Daily 5/CAFÉ, guided reading, published basal series, or any other approach, SPEED™ will compliment how students are able to access vocabulary and practice their word learning strategies in an authentic way. For those who teach Science, Math, or Social Studies, SPEED™ will also help your students access the content and achieve mastery using a goal-driven and performance-based method.

CHAPTER 1
HOW TO USE THIS BOOK

Don't forget that school is a unique place where every teacher is a language teacher and every student is a language learner.

Margo Gottlieb

How to Use This Book:

I know that time is one of the most precious commodities for a teacher. There never seems to be enough of it. So even though the concepts in this book build from one to the next, you can also skip to just the section in this book that addresses your challenge. This book is designed to present a research-based approach to developing vocabulary habits in a way that supports students' interests, needs, and individual levels.

All teachers can benefit from using this type of integrated approach. Still, teachers of English language learners and struggling students have a unique set of challenges. These challenges require a slightly different set of strategies and sequence of learning than others. The strategies and sequences, therefore, have been adapted from the general approach for students who do not receive any language or literacy support.

New teachers and those who are just beginning their journey to include vocabulary instruction into their teaching practice can expect to get the most benefit from reading the book in its entirety since each element is integrated into the full day of instruction. Additionally, veteran teachers who want to enhance their approach to vocabulary instruction would benefit from reading the book from start to finish so that it is clear how each of the strategies and stages in the SPEED Vocabulary Development approach is supported by research and carefully interwoven to provide students with immediate benefits.

I hope that this book offers you a foundation of the research, the strategies, and the resources to impact your students' vocabulary and language needs each and every day.

How the Book Is Organized:

The concepts and strategies that you will find in this book have come from my experiences supporting English language learners and struggling students. The ideas that I share come from these years of teaching, and providing coaching to teachers (that taught in bilingual, dual language, ESL, sheltered, and general education settings). The concepts also stem from having served as an elementary school principal, working as a Director of Educational Supports for some of Chicago's lowest performing schools, visiting hundreds of classrooms, and engaging in thousands of hours of research.

The model is divided into three sections. The first section of the book focuses on why the SPEED™ integrated approach to vocabulary instruction works. Chapter 2 outlines what it means to have vocabulary instruction integrated into the full day of learning. It further shows how to integrate this approach into practices that you are already doing during the course of the day. Chapter 3 explains the five core elements to developing strong academic vocabulary: word consciousness, wide and deep reading and language experiences, explicit instruction in words, explicit instruction in word learning strategies, and explicit instruction in language constructs.

The second section of the book features what this integrated approach looks like in action. Chapter 4 specifies how to select "just right" words for students to learn. Next, chapter 5 details each of the activities in the SPEED™ journal. As part of this chapter, anchor mini-lessons are provided for each activity to help teachers "roll out" or introduce the new strategy or practice. Then throughout the chapters there are examples, or snapshots, of all the anchor charts that support the implementation of the strategies and the approach. It is important to know that while I've given sample scripts for what a model or anchor lesson might look like and sound like, it is not meant to be followed with fidelity. These lessons are flexible and should be adjusted to meet the needs, levels, and interests of your particular students.

The third, and final, section of this book is meant to be a quick resource for those that would like an overview or are short on time. In the Appendix, I outline one way of approaching the first 45 days. These first 45 days are critical to setting up the routines and beginning the important process of building independence in students who may not be used to doing rigorous work independently. However, these first 45 days are also meant to be used flexibly. I encourage you to review the intended outcomes from each roll out lesson from chapter 5 to determine for yourself what components to change and which parts might be beneficial in their original form.

What Is Not in This Book:

There are many foundational practices that build a strong vocabulary base. Choice, motivation, and access to the right materials are just a few. While these practices are not the focus of the book, one critical routine that should be mentioned is actively seeking family involvement.

Know that all families have at least one responsible adult

who wants to be involved in the education of your student. This is true regardless of the student's dominant language, race, economic status, or other defining characteristics. We can all use this truth to help as we problem-solve the three actions in particular: what opportunities are offered to families, how to link family communication to student learning, and ideas that help families learn how to support their students' academic success through college.

When paired with respect and sensitivity, these three factors can open the door to meaningful partnerships between teachers and families.

CHAPTER 2
AN INTEGRATED APPROACH

Think long and move slowly, but always move forward... Change is hard. Change is anxiety-provoking and necessarily slow. When we try to change everything at once, little that matters actually changes.

-Richard Allington

What Is an Integrated Approach?

An integrated approach means giving students varied and interspersed opportunities to learn words and acquire word learning strategies so they are able to continue acquiring and accessing a wide range of words when it is needed the most – which is in context. The only reasonable conclusion then, is that long-term integration means full immersion of these practices into every content area and in the use of all domains of language use and communication. Vocabulary development and language learning then become 365 day a year, school open to close, full-time responsibilities.

Although I never set out to "develop" a framework, I knew I needed to explore how to make this work in a way that was manageable for me as the teacher and for the students I served. I was never afraid of change, especially when I knew that integrated instruction had such incredible benefits for English language learners in particular (Freeman and Freeman, 2007), and struggling students. Yet, I understood that I could not change everything at once as Richard Allington warned.

Over the years, what I've come to appreciate is that integrated vocabulary doesn't have to mean that everything must change now. In fact, if we throw out all the routines that students have learned very little will change. No, integrating is not about making every class English Language Arts. It is about making slow, targeted, and subtle changes over time that have big payoffs in the long run.

So why should you integrate vocabulary instruction into all

aspects of your day? Well, when vocabulary is developed in the content areas, students actually learn the content more effectively. This is because when students encounter challenging words it changes the readability of the text. It makes it harder. This creates more challenges for student comprehension, and leads to difficulty understanding the concepts embedded in the texts. However, when students learn key or essential terms, it provides some language and background knowledge about the subject. This background knowledge serves as the glue to hold additional information that students learn about that topic.

Not only that, but students are able to stay more engaged in the lesson because they are better able to understand the content (Freeman and Freeman, 2007). Think of it this way: Have you ever listened to a book or gone to a presentation or speaker that was way over your head? If you are anything like me then your attention floats in and out of focus. After all, there is little reason to pay attention since you know you won't understand it anyway.

It turns out that students are exactly the same way. The less likely they are to successfully comprehend and find success in a task, the less likely they are to be motivated and willing to engage in challenging and rigorous thinking. The payoffs are simply not great enough for them to invest the mental energy.

Equally important is that integrating vocabulary instruction increases English language learner and struggling students' language and literacy skills. English language learners and struggling students need to engage with rich language in order to learn how to use it. This means that when they are able to read, write, speak, and hear critical vocabulary words in context, the repetition and practice helps to acquire the words and the right times to use them. This allows students to create background knowledge and to use that background knowledge to evaluate their own usage of the target words. This is the beginning stage of word consciousness that will help students learn to be precise in their word choice and vocabulary usage.

1st Steps:

Creating a Language Rich Environment:

One of the simplest steps to begin the process of creating an integrated approach is to increase the amount of rich language displayed throughout the room. A language rich environment serves multiple purposes. It reminds students of the language and vocabulary that has been taught so that it can be used as a resource for students still learning the language and concepts. Language rich environments also serve to reinforce the learning so that there is greater emphasis on the content and language reflected throughout the room. Finally, it serves as a support for boosting students' exposure, which helps provide supplemental support to guided and individualized instruction. Some of the items that can work to create a language rich environment are:

- Interactive word walls
- Anchor charts
- Textbooks
- Student friendly and/or picture dictionaries
- Book displays
- Journals
- Sentence stems and language frames
- Stamina charts
- Student work samples
- Abundant opportunities for discussion and dialogue***

Scheduling Vocabulary into Your Day:

So how can teachers structure their days to include an integrated approach to academic vocabulary instruction? The most logical place to start is with literacy. Whether you use Daily 5, Balanced Literacy, Reading and Writing Workshop, a curriculum series, or any other literacy approach, the literacy block offers plenty of opportunities for students to engage with words.

There are many ways to integrate vocabulary instruction into literacy activities that already exist. One option is to begin the first 30 days of school with short mini-lessons during the literacy block that help build independence. These mini-lessons are outlined in chapters 5 and 7. However, teaching students how to take ownership of their vocabulary development helps lessen the need to create a separate time in addition to all the other responsibilities that teachers already have. While we describe the framework for using the SPEED™ approach in detail later in the book, some actions teachers can begin taking today are listed below.

- When lesson planning, list the vocabulary needed the master the content
- Review reading materials before assigning reading to students
- Front loading vocabulary before starting a read aloud
- Model using the vocabulary taught when giving directions and talking about the content
- Posting vocabulary words on a word wall
- Have students write and collect new vocabulary words when they read

- Provide students with lots of opportunities to use new words in all four domains of language (reading, writing, speaking, and listening)
- Provide language frames and sentence stems to guide and support vocabulary usage
- Celebrate students' use of precise vocabulary as often as possible

The actions listed above are steps any teacher can take to begin addressing academic vocabulary right now. While we have listed them in the context of literacy instruction, the truth is that the exact same actions are practical and valuable for content area instruction, too. Math, Science, Social Studies, and other content area textbooks also have a great deal of reading, writing, speaking, and listening tasks. Giving students the opportunity to learn the vocabulary needed to be successful in those tasks is one great way to help them be successful.

Personalizing Learning:

Another component of the SPEED™ framework is the individualization of the learning. This gives every student the opportunity to follow their own unique word learning path that meets their literacy and language needs. If we don't give all students the same books to read independently, it only seems logical that we wouldn't approach vocabulary instruction in a "one size fits all" manner.

ELLs and struggling students come with their own interests, strengths, and learning opportunities. This framework shows teachers how to train their students to know what words to collect, understand, and apply. The set of words each student is expected to master is different because the interests, strengths, and opportunities for growth are different for each of them. This choice, ownership, and personalization are all part of what makes the learning "stick."

The Routine:

The routine for vocabulary acquisition that is presented here allows students to get comfortable while still allowing for variety and novelty. Students have the opportunity to engage in meaningful activities that are designed help them deepen their understanding of each word they study. But it also supports teachers in the introduction of new vocabulary words.

The teacher routine, which is outlined below, is the process for whole group instruction. It is best used when the text is written at grade level even though your students may not have a grade-level vocabulary. Because of the process, this routine also allows students to move forward in their study of "teacher choice" words with confidence and independence. The teacher routine for literacy and all content areas is as follows:

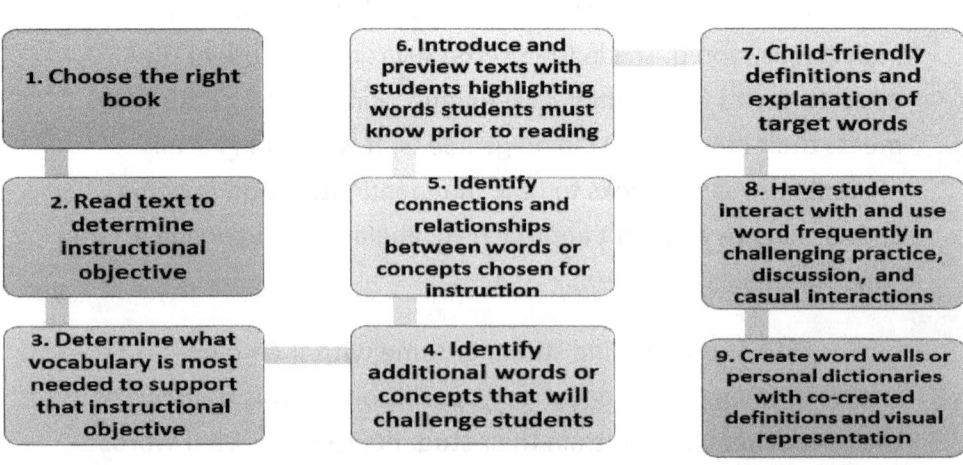

Figure 2.1 – Routine for planning integrated vocabulary instruction

In addition to the teacher routine, the student practices listed below support student mastery of the vocabulary words:

Research-based instructional practices that deepen vocabulary acquisition

1. Draw on **background knowledge**
2. Think about **why** they believe what they do as they encounter new words
3. **Notice** things about words
4. **Predict** and infer meanings
5. **Question** the use of specific words in print and speech
6. **Analyze** words and parts of words
7. **Evaluate** their own use of new words and the words used by others
8. Identifying **synonyms** and **antonyms**
9. Looking for roots and using **cognates**
10. **Connecting** new words to known words
11. **Practice strategies** for learning words that can be applied in any context
12. Frequently use new vocabulary in **discussion** and even casual interactions
13. Be a part of creating word walls with **co-created definitions** and **visual representations**

> 14. Introduce words through the **context** of authentic children's texts
> 15. Work to author **child-friendly definitions** and explanation of target words
> 16. Find **examples** of how words are used in other contexts

Figure 2.2 Instructional practices designed to foster vocabulary mastery

CHAPTER 3

THE 5 ELEMENTS OF VOCABULARY INSTRUCTION FOR ELLS AND STRUGGLING LEARNERS

Thus it can be argued that there is no knowledge addressed in school in which application is more crucial than knowledge of word meanings.

Anderson &Nagy (1991)

The Five Core Elements of Vocabulary Instruction:

If you think about vocabulary development as one of the critical components of literacy instruction, then it is important to know how to both define and identify its core elements. Specifically for EL's and struggling learners, there are 5 core elements of vocabulary instruction across all content areas. They are word consciousness, opportunities to engage in a wide range of literacy and language experiences, explicit instruction in academic words, explicit instruction in word learning strategies, and explicit instruction in the academic language of the discipline. In the next sections, we will briefly describe each.

The 1st Element –

Word Consciousness:

> *Really knowing a word... always means being able to apply it flexibly but accurately in a wide range of new contexts and situations. Thus it can be argued that there is no knowledge addressed in school in which application is more crucial than knowledge of word meanings. The challenge for educators is to provide instruction of the sort that will lead to flexible application of word knowledge.*
>
> *Anderson & Nagy (1991)*

These words have always stood out to me as incredibly important. An obvious struggle when teaching students vocabulary is to help learners understand this single, and essential, truth -- words matter. And to know a word, does not mean to recite a dictionary definition. Those rarely help students to apply it when needed most. The focus must be on students' ability to apply the words that they acquire, while adapting their knowledge and ability to use these words as new contexts and situations arise.

Word consciousness is comprised of three parts:

1. **Awareness of words and word learning strategies –**

    Do students know what they don't know? Do they recognize new words when they arise, and do students know what to do with these words? Awareness of words and word learning strategies is the part of word consciousness that tells a student to stop and pay attention to something new. The awareness is what allows each student the mindfulness to begin the process of stopping, problem solving with the new word, and assimilating the new knowledge gained from that interaction. It is awareness that gets students to notice and then respond to a new word. Without awareness, no meaningful and authentic action can or will take place on the part of the learner.

2. **Appreciation for and enjoyment of words and word learning –**

    Do students know why words are important? Do they recognize how they use words, the power that they hold, and difference they can have on the result of communication? Appreciation provides students with a reason and motivation to engage in the hard work of learning more than 3,000 new vocabulary words each year. In addition, we intrinsically know and are supported by research that learning experiences that are fun, novel, and allow students to feel successful actually change the chemistry of the brain. This happens by making students more focused, smarter, more confident, and more aggressive in their attempt to assimilate new words. This helps students apply their new learning in search of more fun and more success. The effect is as strong as any drug. And the more you experience joy and success, the more students will go on to win. This science applies to word learning in that students must see how it is fun and experience success in using new words if they are to "buy in." With buy in, students are more motivated to be engaged in such challenging work, even if it's hard.

3. **The ability to make connections between words and extend word knowledge to new encounters –**

Do students know how and when to use these words beyond the initial encounter during a lesson or when reading a text? Can students see how new words are connected to words that might already exist in their vocabularies? Are students actively noticing these words in books or other forms of communication? Have they intentionally worked to assimilate these words into their regular academic speech? Connecting and extending word knowledge is what characterizes the purpose of vocabulary instruction. This part of word consciousness really addresses the broad application and prolonged understanding of a word that embodies what it means to truly know a word. For this reason, to make connections is to continue expanding the ways in which a word can be used, combined, and presented in order to impact the overall experience with communication.

Teacher Model	Word Rich Environment and Literature	Word Play	Games
• Attention to the skillful use of words in texts • Their own choice of words • Motivating students to recognize how words are used and where they appear outside of class • Encouraging students to expand their own range of word choice in their speech and writing	• Dictionaries • Thesauruses • Word walls • Word games • Word puzzles • Literature and poetry books • Word play books • Joke books	• Active, social, learning that provides motivation to improve their language skills • *Names*: eponyms, toponyms • *Expressions*: proverbs, slang • *Word formations*: acronyms, portmanteaus • *Word games*: puns, riddles, tongue twisters • *Word manipulations*: anagrams, palindromes	• Word Trees • Vocabulary Jeopardy • Part Relays • Vocabul-opoly • Word Creation • Go Fish • Scavenger Hunt • Bingo • Pictionary • 20 Questions

Figure 3.1 - Strategies for building word consciousness

The 2nd Element –

Opportunities to engage in a wide range of literacy and language experiences:

Most of the language we have learned is acquired incidentally, by engaging in a range of literacy and language activities that take place throughout the day (Graves, 2013). This is one of many reasons that the language and literacy experiences we design for kids matter. Limiting ELLs access or exposure to rich language and reading experiences only delays and impedes students' ability to acquire the necessary words. Access to vocabulary translates to access to the content standards as well as growth as readers and writers.

During the course of the day there is a range of reading, literacy, and language experiences we can offer students in order to facilitate their vocabulary development and incidental word learning. However, it takes intentional planning of the learning objective. It also requires consideration of the background knowledge that each learner brings. This process allows teachers to effectively match the range of opportunities that is right for the students and unit of learning.

Independent Reading

Independent reading allows students to read books that they've chosen while the teacher provides targeted instruction to small groups or confers with individuals (Fountas & Pinnell, 2001). During independent reading, students are able to increase the amount of time they spend engaged in reading practice. This practice can be an extension of the mini-lesson. However, it can also be a time where students are practicing the strategies that have been taught during guided reading and/or one-on-one conferences.

While we will not get into the details of setting up independent reading, some notable components are the reading level of the text selected – for the independent reading level, students should be able to read the text with 95% - 100% accuracy with comprehension (Fountas & Pinnell, 2009). There are a number of ways to calculate reading accuracy, but one easy and accessible way for students to own this process is to use the "five finger rule." With the five finger rule, students can open any book they are interested in reading. Students then hold up a finger every time they encounter a word that they do not know. If there are no new words, then they know that the book is too easy for them. When they reach 2-3 fingers, they know that the book is "just right" for them. When they reach 4 fingers (meaning 4 unknown words), they know that the book is alright for them to try if they are really motivated and interested in reading about the topic or characters. Once they reach 5 fingers, they know that the book is too difficult for independent reading.

For vocabulary instruction, independent reading is a great time for students to collect words for their own vocabulary development. While we will discuss the vocabulary journals in later chapters, independent reading books allow students to jot down words that they don't know while they are reading. This gives them the opportunity to then explore these words in depth later during the literacy block. One reason independent reading is so effective for word collecting is that students gain exposure to a variety of genres of their choosing which provides access to the terminology of that genre. By learning the "construct" of the genre, students expand their vocabularies and expand their word base. For example, my daughter knew the term "evolve" from reading Pokemon at a very young age. She learned it, because it is a term regularly used in that series or genre.

5 Finger Rule

0-1 = Too Easy
2-3 = *Just Right*
4 = OK to Try
5 = Too Hard

Figure 3.2 - 5 Finger Rule anchor chart

Read Alouds

Read alouds may occur in any content area. Reading aloud to ELLs and struggling students provides a key scaffold for oral language development and provides many benefits for comprehension (Snow, Burns, & Griffin, 1998). For ELLs and struggling students, read alouds and shared reading give them the opportunity to be exposed to rich language that includes words they might not encounter when reading independently. It also allows students to access more complex content because of the supports and scaffolds provided by the teacher. One reason for this is because many students are able to comprehend (provided there is comprehensible input) more when listening than what they are able to comprehend when engaging in the very complex task of reading.

There are a number of factors to consider when choosing a book and the right words to highlight in a read aloud. The three most important considerations are the objective of the read aloud, the background knowledge of the students, and the vocabulary words embedded in the text that need to be taught. The objective of the read aloud will determine the right book to be read. Whether fiction or informational, leveled or at grade level, the range of text types chosen should coincide with its instructional purpose.

Another important consideration is the background knowledge needed to understand the read aloud. One way to think about background knowledge is to ask yourself what you already need to know in order to understand the text. For example, if I see a picture of a snowman in a book, I may use my background knowledge to infer that this story is taking place in the wintertime even though it is not explicitly stated. This is because I know that snowmen are made of snow, which falls during the winter, and a snowman can only remain during the coldest months of the year. However, this background knowledge comes from my personal experiences building snowmen while living in the Chicagoland area. As teachers, it helps to challenge our assumptions of what background knowledge and universal experiences our students have, especially when working with ELLs and struggling students. One never knows when you'll encounter a student who's never seen a snowman before and has no background knowledge from which to draw.

The third consideration is the challenging words that students will need to learn in order to understand the text being read. Since read alouds leverage students' oral language, which tends to more developed, teachers have the opportunity to select texts that are full of rich vocabulary beyond students' independent reading level. This exposure helps to increase students' individual word knowledge, but not if the students are not supported during the interaction with the words. One way of supporting students is through the cognitively challenging talk that takes place both before and after the read aloud.

There are two categories of words that can pose a challenge to students during a read aloud. One is incidental or supplementary words that are not necessary for understanding the main idea and important concepts. These are words that a teacher might quickly explain on the spot or foreshadow for students prior to beginning the reading.

The second category of words are those that I call the "essential terms." Essential terms are those critical words and concepts that are fundamental to a student's comprehension of the text or concept as a whole. Essential terms are so crucial because they represent a basic connection between the specific word chosen by the author and the concept, mood, or enduring understanding of the reading itself. These essential terms are words that teachers should identify beforehand in order to provide explicit instruction.

Guided Reading

Guided reading is one form of small group instruction where teachers have the opportunity to provide one strategy, skill, or teach point that is intended to improve the students' ability to read independently. "The purpose of guided reading is to enable children to use and develop strategies 'on the run.' ...They (students) focus primarily on constructing meaning while using problem-solving strategies to figure out words they don't know, deal with tricky sentence structure, and understand concepts or ideas they have not previously met in print." (Fountas & Pinnell, 2001).

Guided reading uses students' instructional reading level in order to provide students with the opportunity to practice key strategies that allow them to access increasingly more complex texts. This is done by keeping students in the zone of proximal development. The zone of proximal development (Vygotsky, 1978), is the learning and growth students can experience with focused support by the teacher. This is done by having students focus on and work with appropriately challenging texts then gradually releasing teacher support in order to understand more clearly, read more productively, and problem solve the unknown words they encounter.

Since guided reading helps small group of students develop their comprehension and problem-solving strategies, it is one of many chances that teachers have to help students work through issues that may arise during their vocabulary development and word work. For instance, if you notice that students are not stopping when they encounter new and unknown words, the teacher can provide targeted and focused instruction on a specific strategy for tackling that issue. This targeted instruction might include teaching students to stop when they encounter a word they don't know, rather than just continuing to read the selection. Then additional strategies can be taught in order for them to know how to approximate the meaning of the unknown word using a number of word clues and context clues. For more information on the actual strategies for word learning and strategies for teaching the academic language of the discipline, see *The Academic Vocabulary Book: Strategies for English Learners and Struggling Students*, (Guilamo, June 2016).

Content Areas Instruction

Instruction in Math, Science, Social Studies, and all other content areas is full of reading tasks. The texts that accompany these disciplines are usually based on grade level gradients, regardless of the reading level of the class you serve.

Content area texts are also full of tier two and tier three vocabulary words that may call for explicit instruction in the meaning of those words. While there are many ways of defining the three tiers of vocabulary, the way that always helped me to learn them was to think of tier one as everyday words that students use like the word *love*. Tier two are the fancier versions of words and concepts that students might already know like the word *adoration*. Tier three are the domain-specific words of a discipline like the term *aortic chamber*.

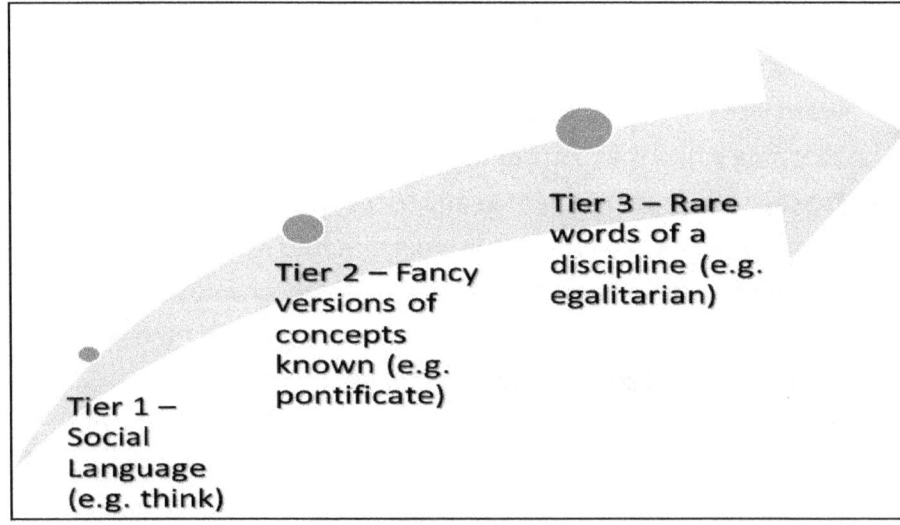

Figure 3.3 - Three tiers of vocabulary

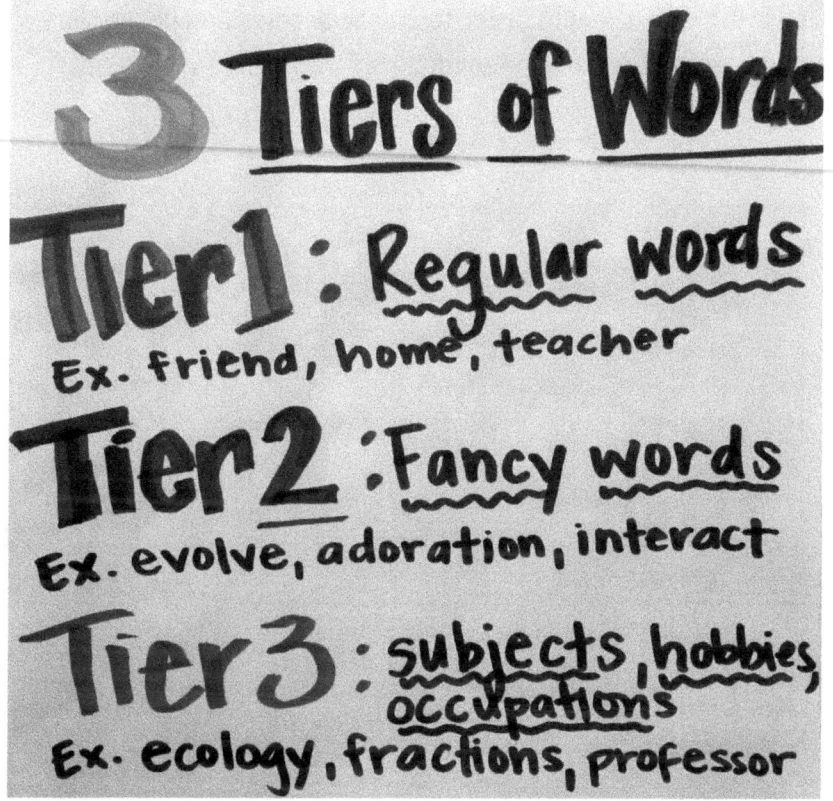

Figure 3.4 – Three tiers of vocabulary anchor chart

Background Knowledge

Again, teachers who serve ELLs and struggling students will need to be cautious when planning instruction and language experiences as the range in background knowledge is enormous within this population of students. Not all ELLs and struggling students have been exposed to the same tier one vocabulary, which creates an additional challenge when helping students develop their tier two and tier three vocabulary foundations. Once more, this is why approaching vocabulary development with SPEED™ is important. Since students start with a unique reading level and vocabulary base, it is important to honor the knowledge they bring with them in order to create accelerated vocabulary learning using their own individualized path.

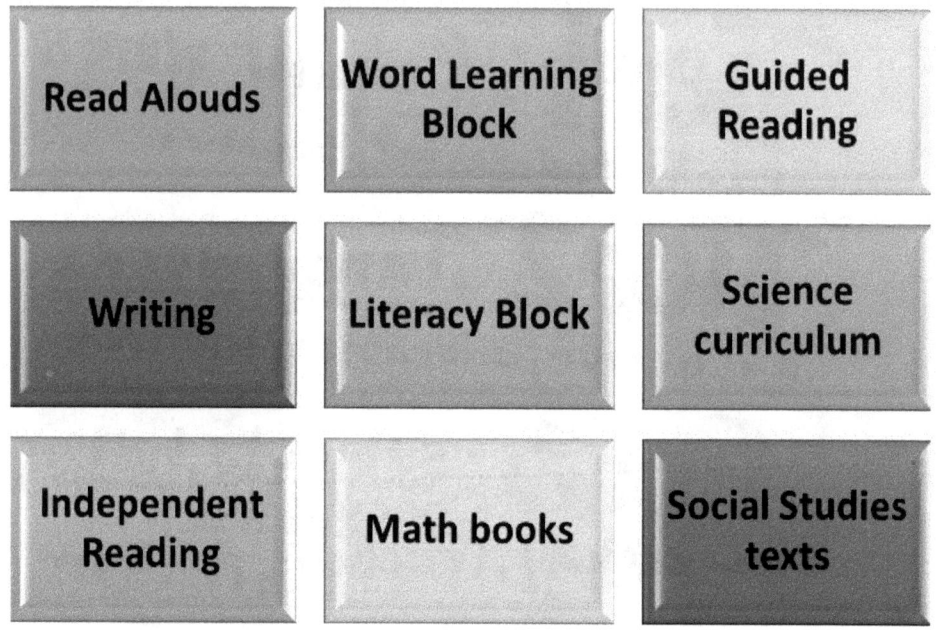

Figure 3.5 - Opportunities for reading a wide range of texts

There are many other opportunities for students to engage with a wide range of texts, literacy, and language experiences. By carefully guiding the daily interaction with these varied texts and language experiences, we can increase in students' generative word knowledge as they are exposed to rich oral language in addition to wide reading (Graves, 2000).

Challenging Talk

A vital opportunity to shape the language experience and interaction with reading activities is to build in time for challenging and metacognitive talk. This type of "accountable talk" gives students a chance to talk about what strategies they are using as they read, and why they chose that strategy for what they are tackling as a learner. This type of challenging talk can be done as part of a one-on-one conference, small group instruction, or as a whole class discussion or share out. The key is providing ELLs and struggling students with opportunities for deep and challenging dialogue that helps students do more than just get the right answer. This dialogue and "talk" must be aimed at making their thinking visible in order to understand how they are doing and where they are situated in the learning process.

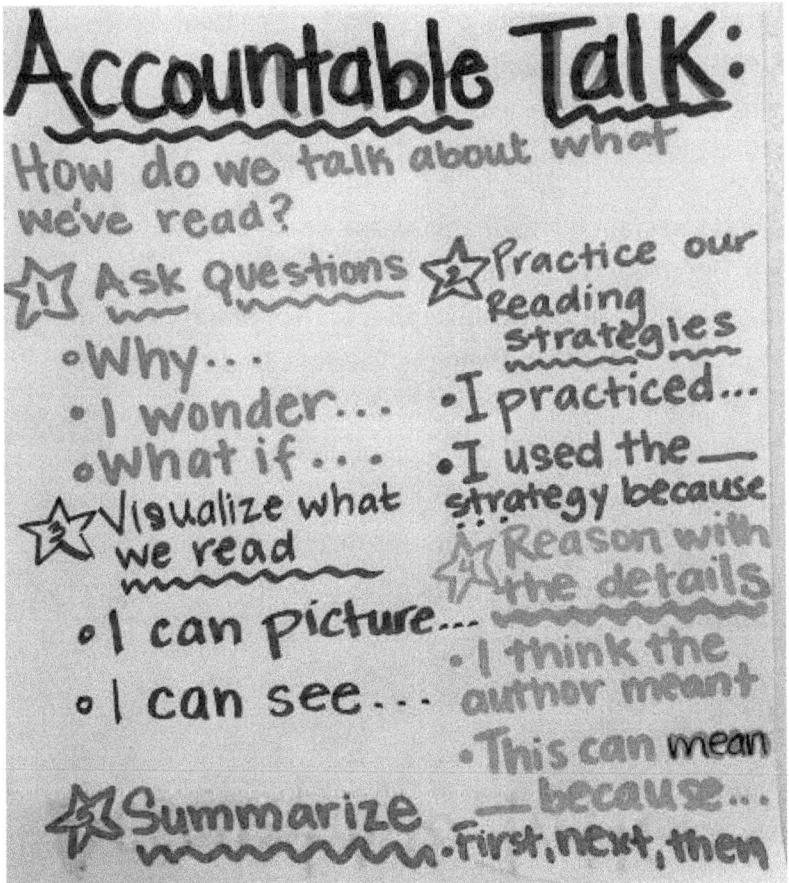

Figure 3.6 – Challenging and accountable talk sentence starters

The 3rd Element –

Explicit instruction in academic words:

The 3rd element when developing vocabularies with ELLs and struggling students is the explicit instruction they receive around particular words that all must know. Even though every student enters class with their own vocabulary foundation, there are times when the entire class needs to know the same term. With the arrival of the common core state standards, this need to have a common vocabulary has become even more important to integrate as part of students' overall learning routine. Teachers can do this by being careful in the selection of words to teach, matching teaching strategies, and intentionally coordinating processing and ownership.

When selecting words that ELLs and struggling students have to know, one factor to take into consideration is the benefit of learning the word on the achievement of the learning objective of the lesson. In the previous element, we discussed the idea of "essential terms." As a reminder, essential terms are the most significant words that students need to understand the text or concept as a whole. For example, when working on a unit about fractions, some of the essential terms might be fraction, part, and whole. Without understanding the real, conceptual, and nuanced meaning of these words, students will struggle during the entire unit.

Essential terms are not just domain specific words, or tier three words. There are a number of words that are essential for students' overall success, including "thinking" words. These are the words that communicate the depth of knowledge (Webb and others, 2005) students are expected to practice during a given activity. They also frame language objectives for students who are learning English. Recite, define, categorize, explain, create, reflect – these are all thinking words. The value of taking the time to ensure that everyone has a shared and mutual understanding of what these words mean is invaluable. Doing so provides students with opportunities to know what successfully achieving the objective looks and sounds like.

There are a number of strategies teachers can use when introducing new vocabulary. The SPEED™ approach sequences a variety of activities designed to balance the research and application of vocabulary development and language acquisition. But the activities included are not meant to be a complete list of all the possibilities. Some additional strategies that are incredibly powerful for ELLs and struggling students are listed below.

Total Physical Response

Total physical response (TPR) was developed by James Asher (1977). It was made to link language and communication with physical movement just like in the game charades. By assigning physical movements to language, students can quickly see the words in action, helping them to acquire the vocabulary, grammar, and other structures of language. The reason this approach works with this group of students, and young children in particular, is that language and words are mostly learned by using receptive language (listening) and when stress is low. When students are able to see the words and concepts in action using this game-like approach, students are able to lower their defenses, leverage both sides of their brains, and retain the visualization that stays with them.

Visual Representations

Another strategy is to use visual representations, icons, symbols, realia, movies, maps, charts, and other images that create strong connections in the brain. As human beings, we learn by connecting ideas to visuals to create pictures in our minds. Our minds are like cameras that are constantly recording. When we include pictures as part of that recording, it makes it easier to replay the movie. For example, if you are given a series of numbers (1, 2, 2, 1, 2, 10, 4, 2) to remember, you might be able to do it. But what if I show you a picture with arrows pointing at 1 head, 2 eyes, 2 ears, 1 mouth, 2 arms, 10 fingers, 4 major bones in your legs, and 2 feet? Does the task become much simpler?

Even more, our brains are constantly connecting memories to our senses. A smell can cause us to think of an important moment in our lives. A song can take us back to a momentous event. But vision is the most powerful of the senses. Commercials count on it. A simple swoop can make us think of going on a run. A golden arch can help us to recall an entire menu. And anchoring a new word or concept in the right image or symbol can have the same potent effect by creating background knowledge where none exists or allowing students to connect that image to something they already know.

Concept Mapping

One last, valuable strategy that I'll share is concept mapping. Concept mapping is one of many forms of word association. Associations help students learn more about a word or concept by exploring prior knowledge about related ideas and words. Most students use spider web graphic organizers to help them organize the map of their ideas, but this is not necessary.

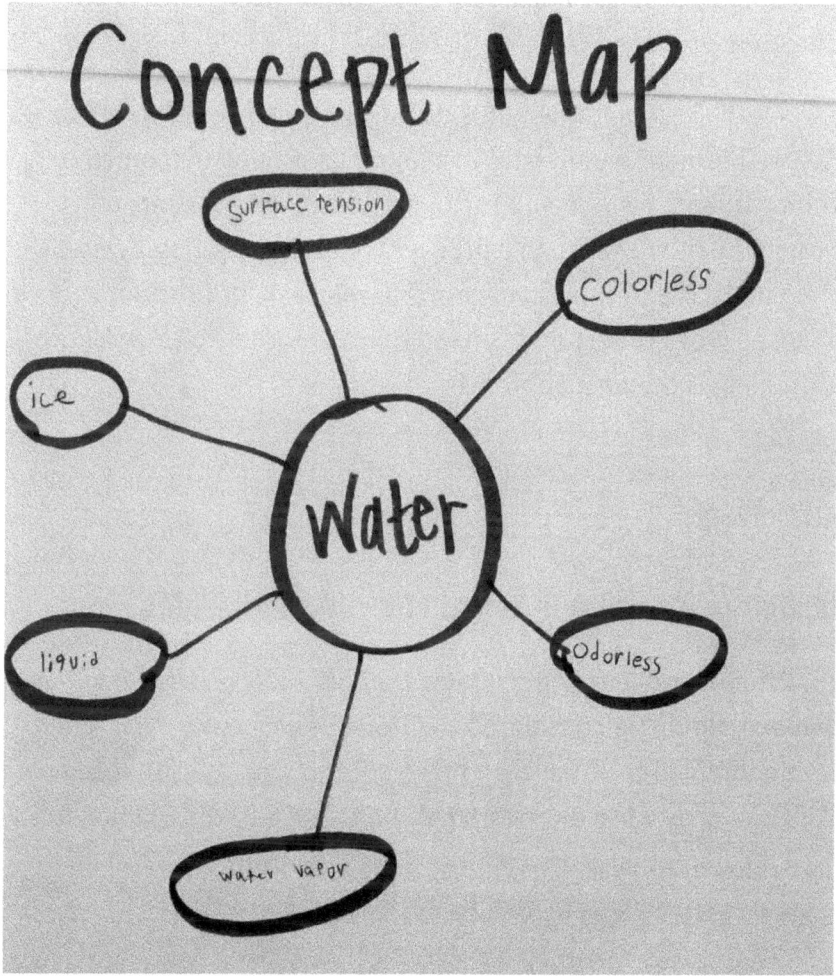

Figure 3.7 – Example concept map

Student Ownership

The remaining question is how to balance student processing with student ownership. In other words, when is it right to give ELLs and struggling students the opportunity to engage in healthy struggle versus when is it right to scaffold instruction? The full answer is complicated and the subject of *The Academic Vocabulary Book: Strategies for English Learners and Struggling Students*, Guilamo 2016.

But, in short, when introducing a new concept that is an essential term of a unit, studies support improved outcomes when students have the opportunity to explore the concept through healthy challenge paired with visual clues. However, when there is a new procedure, academic task, or functional language word that students need to use in order to take action, scaffolding is the best approach.

The 4th Element –

Explicit Instruction in Word Learning Strategies

While word learning strategies cannot exist on their own, this element should be considered the heart of vocabulary development. This is because these are the strategies that allow students to take the desire from the 1st element, the reading from the 2nd element, and the common language from the 3rd element to create meaning from additional unknown words they encounter.

There are 3 key types of word learning strategies that ELLs and struggling students might use. Interlingual clues (Haastrup, 1989) are clues students pull from their knowledge of other languages. Context clues are clues students pull from the surrounding words, sentences, story, and their own general knowledge. Lastly, morphemic clues are those that students pull from different parts of the word itself.

Interlingual Clues - Cognates

For students who speak another language, cognate study can be a great source of knowledge. Cognates are words that share the same linguistic family (Molina, 2011). Cognates are powerful tools for ELLs because they share similar pronunciation, spelling patterns, and meaning. These words allow ELLs to use their vocabulary foundation from their native language to be transferred over to English. When taught how to use cognates, many ELLs (especially those speaking Spanish (Baumann, Edwars, Boland, & Font, 2012)) are able grow what they know in English by transferring the ideas they already had in another language. This asset-based approach to teaching can only help to build a strong vocabulary base.

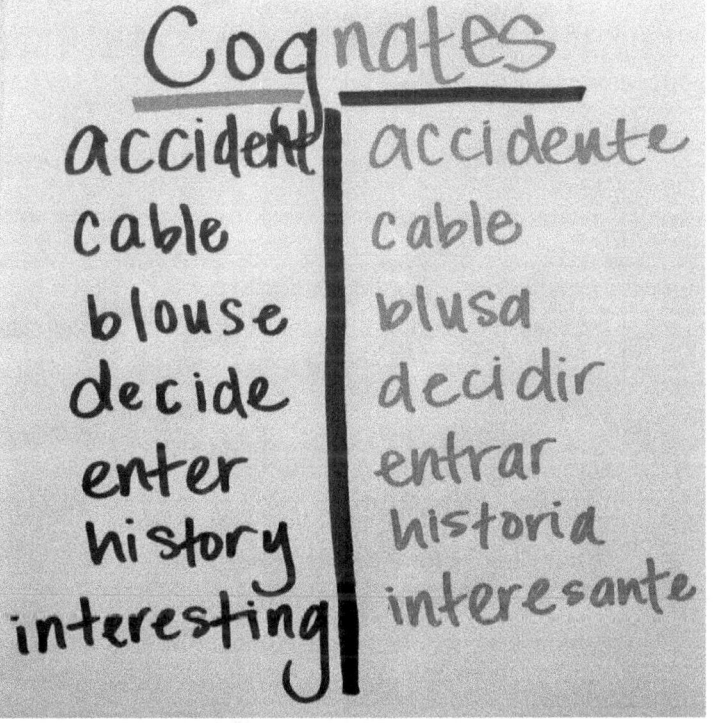

Figure 3.8 – Example cognate anchor chart

Context Clues

Context clues help readers to infer the meaning of words by using the surrounding words, phrases, sentences, story, and combing them with one's own background knowledge. However, since context clues use knowledge of text structure, grammar, language conventions, and background knowledge, it is very difficult for ELLs and struggling students. There are generally 6 types of context clues. Each context clue also comes with its own signal words that should clue the reader as to the type of context clue the author has chosen to use. The table below outlines the 6 types of context clues. They are listed in order of the most common and easiest to learn to the most complex. When teaching context clues, it is important to teach them one at a time – not so that they can master which type is which, but so that they are able to feel confident as they work to apply each one of them successfully.

Context Clue	Signal Words	Example	Text types
1. Definition	Is defined as, means, that is, look for boldface or italics	The Chicago Art Museum **vernissage**, that is their gallery reception, lasted till almost midnight.	Largely informational texts
2. Example	For example, for instance, look for a phrase surrounded by commas	For instance, large gymnasiums, banquet halls, and open concept houses are very commodious.	All

3. Synonym	Or, in other words, also known as, sometimes called	When Joseph was running, his <u>cognomen</u>, or nickname, was wingman.	All
4. Antonym	But, however, in contrast, instead of, unlike, yet, as opposed to, on the contrary	Fabiola is a <u>wordmonger</u>, unlike you who are thoughtful with the words you choose.	All
5. Compare and contrast	Same as, similar, alike, both, instead of, different from, as opposed to	Some plants are <u>rupestrine</u> and thrive in mountains, as opposed to others that survive best in lush forest areas.	Largely informational text: historical, scientific, etc.
6. General	Look for information that is familiar to you because the author uses a number of clue words and phrases that support the meaning.	The **<u>florilegium</u>**, or collection of stories, is similar to the old anthology that the English department used to use.	All

Figure 3.9 – Six types of context clues

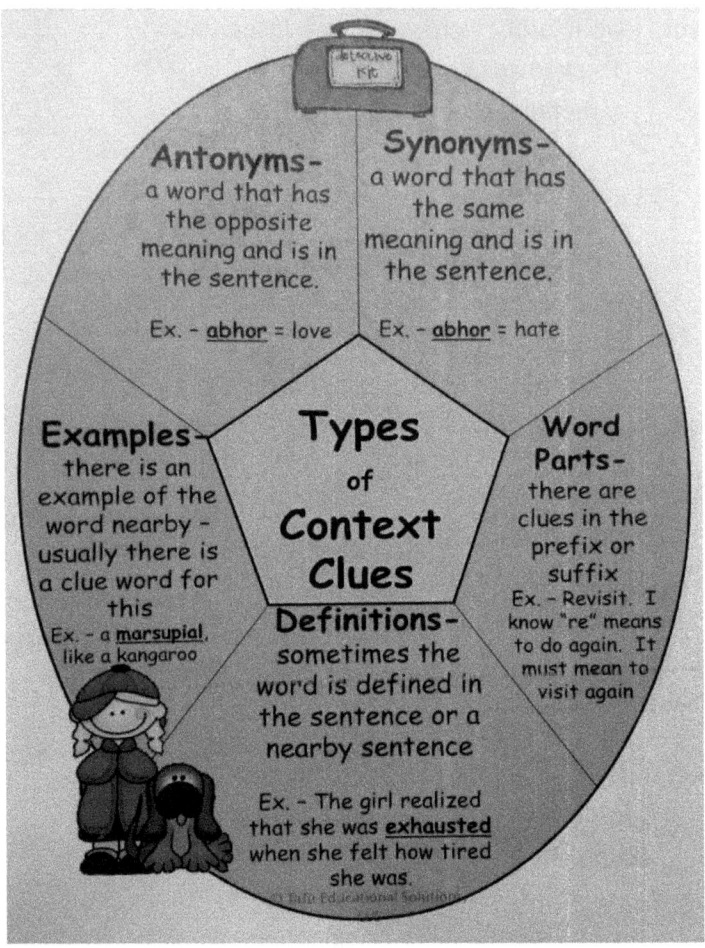

Figure 3.10 – Context clue student reference page

There are a number of strategies to teach the various context clues. However, all strategies should include these 5 components:

1. What the context clue is
2. What an example is
3. Which texts use those clues

4. What the signal words are
5. What to do when you see the signals

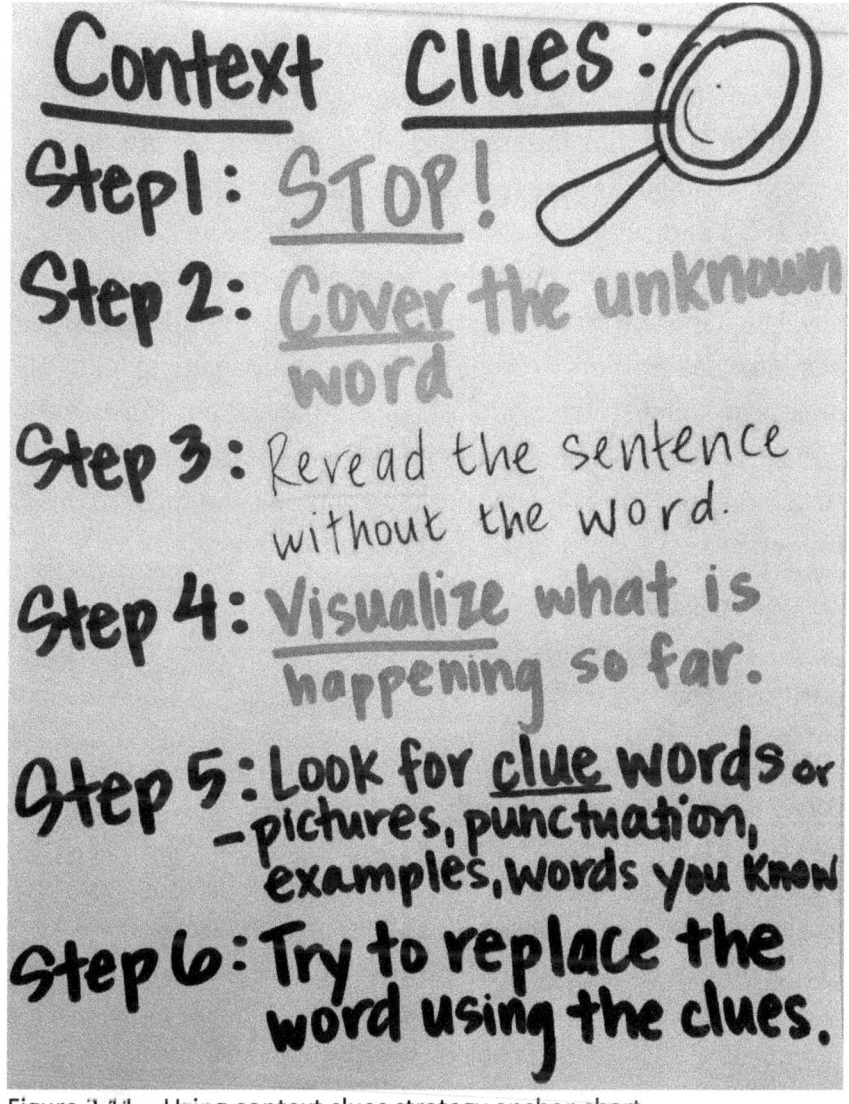

Figure 3.11 – Using context clues strategy anchor chart

The 5th Element –

Explicit Instruction in the Academic Language of the Discipline

Academic language is the language that helps students be successful in learning the standards. It is made up of both the words and language structures needed to be a part of the learning task and a part of the assessment of that task, as well. Academic language is something not only needed by students learning a new language and struggling students, but it is something that is needed by all learners in order to support their ability to hold precise academic conversations and communication. The essential parts of academic language are the language objectives, language structures, and the academic vocabulary that is the focus of this framework.

Language Objectives

Language objectives tell students how they will learn the content and express what language functions they will use in order to participate in the learning. In order for teachers to plan for the language objective, they must first know their students. What are students' language levels, reading levels, and abilities? The answers to these questions pave the way for teachers to be able to match the right language objectives and supports. What is the right match? One that maintains high expectations while supporting the range of expressive (produce) and receptive (comprehend) language students have mastered (Vogt & Echevarria, 2008).

There is still a lot of debate as to whether content objectives should be written in student-friendly language. However, language objectives do not have the same controversy. They should always be in student-friendly language. This helps students understand what they are going to be able to learn and do. Because of the fact that they are action-oriented, students must understand what it is that they are expected to do.

Also, language objective should be delivered in writing and orally. The multiple exposure achieves a number of goals. It allows students to read the language objective and have a place to refer back to. Students who have greater oral language are able to hear the language objective so that they too can understand well enough to take the action outlined. Finally, it serves as a kind of agenda and self-assessment for teachers and students to refer back to during the review to see if they indeed learned and were able to take the action listed in the objective. This is great real-time information for teachers who want to pull small groups of students who were not able to master the language or content objective.

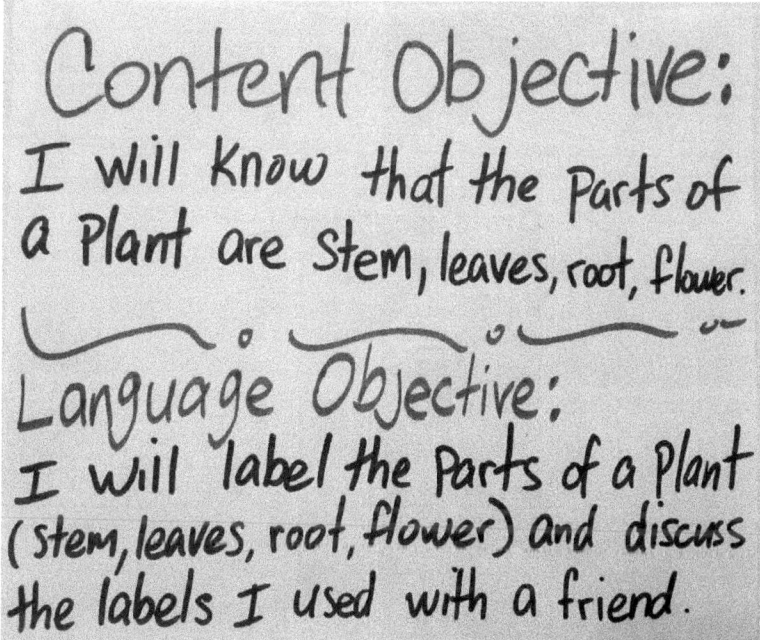

Figure 3.12 – Content and language objectives

Language Structures

Language structures are driven by grammar, conventions, and word order. The graph below shows one example of how we can support students in their use of grade level and academic language structures. By using these types of language frames, teachers can guide and direct academic conversations by providing support, and step out of the conversation to provide independence and ownership at the same time.

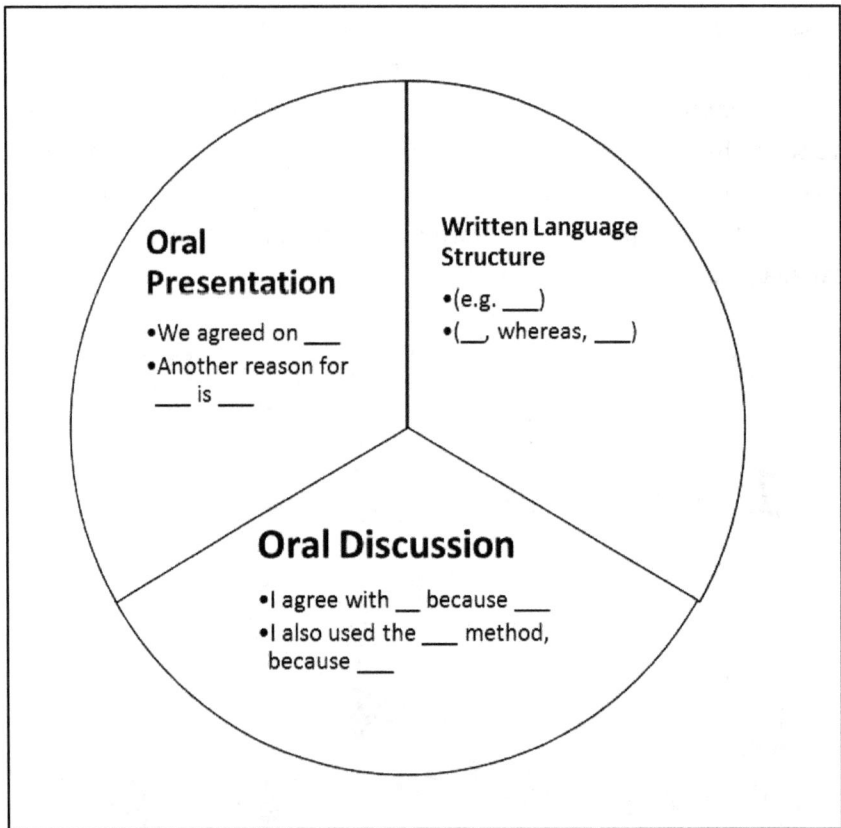

Figure 3.13 - Language structures

If we want to accelerate learning, then the supports that teachers provide should pair the structure that makes the task complex with the language proficiency of the students. Based on these factors, teachers can make calculated decisions about how to differentiate and scaffold the learning experience. Some of the structures that make language complex for students are listed below. This is not a complete list of all possible structures, nor should it be used to change everything at once. But it is a place to begin looking when planning instruction.

Structures	Conventions	Word Order	Forms
Tenses	Showing possession	Sequencing adjectives	Use of visuals
Conditional forms	Punctuation	Prepositional phrases	Pronoun usage
Verb forms	Spelling	Subordinate clauses	Sentence type – compound & complex
Syntax	Capitalization		
Context	Consistency in paragraphs	Relative clauses	

Figure 3.14 – Elements of language complexity

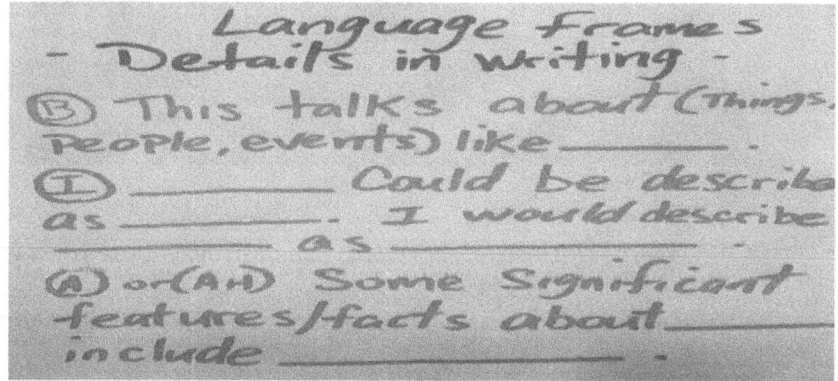

Figure 3.15 – Language frames to support academic language use

CHAPTER 4

SELECTING "JUST RIGHT" VOCABULARY TO ACQUIRE

Words can inspire. And words can destroy. Choose yours well.

Robin Sharma

Selecting "Just Right" Vocabulary:

Thorough vocabulary development can be incredibly influential in supporting reading, comprehension, and overall academic achievement. SPEED™ provides a structured way for students to collect words of their choosing and work with words identified as critical by the teacher to practice the knowledge of these words and practice their skill in using them.

Picking Just Right Words				
Student Choice		**Teacher Choice**		
Content	**Function**	**Content**	**Function**	
Juicy	Unknown	**Essential** (tier 3 discipline specific)	Instrumental	Imaginative
Unknown	Transitional	**Standards-based** (general academic)	Regulatory	Heuristic

Repeating	Connected to L1	**Thinking** (language objective terms)	Interactional	Representational
		Connected (highest-frequency words)	Personal	

Figure 4.1 – Overview of picking "Just Right" Words

Student Choice

When we focus on student choice words, the process starts by teaching students to learn what makes a word worth picking. While there are a number of methods for making that choice, I've listed three that can be very impactful and easy for students to remember. These three are picking words that are "juicy," words that are unknown, and words that repeat in any form.

Juicy Words

I start my classes out by talking about why it is important to learn new words. I use students' background knowledge by asking them to turn and talk to a partner about a time that they learned something new. What about it made them want to learn that new thing? I then relate that to learning new words. "What was the last truly new word you've learned?" I ask. We do a word splash of words that the students call out. We close by talking about choosing to learn new words to grow and explore new things, and choosing to learn new words to communicate with others so that you're not alone in your silence.

The next day, the class and I talk about what makes a word so "juicy" that it is worth them collecting and adding to their own collections of vocabulary. We do this by reading the book *Max's Words* (Banks, 2006). In this book, Max has two brothers who have great collections of stamps and coins. The problem is that neither will share their collections with their brother. So Max decides that he is going to start collecting words. Max starts with a small collection of simple words, but then it grows into a beautiful and imaginative collection that helps him to build stories.

After I read the story, we create a class definition for "juicy" words. Some of the responses included the following:

- Helps you to visualize something
- Remind you of something
- Its sounds fun to say it
- I never heard it used that way
- It makes you feel something different after you read it or hear it

I then ask them to search the room. "Find the juiciest words in your book bins and around the room that help to tell your story. Write them down on the notecards on your desk. Know that we will share how these juicy words tell your story." Students excitedly go around the room looking for words to tell about how they came to this country, how they struggled and overcame challenges in life, and how they basked in the joyous moments of their lives. They've got it – words matter.

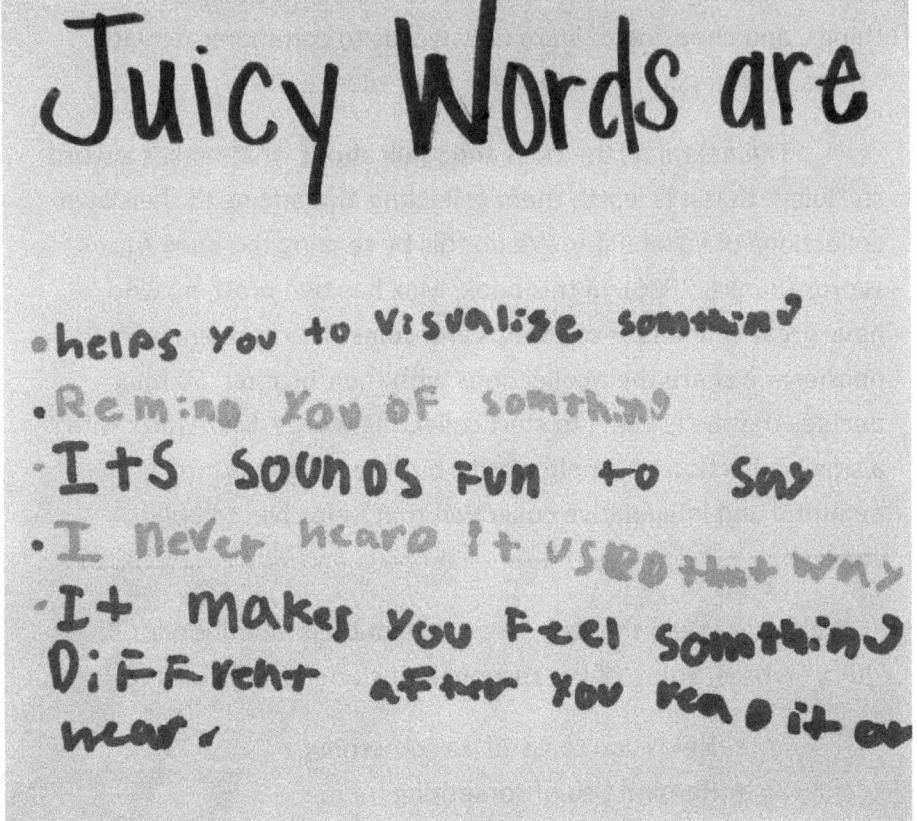

Figure 4.2 – Student brainstorm of juicy words

Unknown Words

The next lesson focuses on collecting unknown words. I ask them, "What is an unknown word? Turn and talk to your partner." Students turn and discuss what they think the word means. I move throughout the room listening in and saying the phrase, "I think unknown means..." and prompting them with "... because..." Giving my students this language to push the conversation and to use complete sentences is vital.

After about 3 minutes, we share out. "I heard some very thoughtful conversations about what an unknown word might mean. I need four volunteers to share what you and your partner talked about." Most of the hands go up, and I call the four names of the students who will share. Again, I do this so that students have time to mentally prepare what they are going to say, which helps to decrease their anxiety levels.

Here are some of the ideas that were shared as part of that process:

- New word
- New ideas
- Strange
- Different
- Not the same
- Uncommon

I then ask if they know what really great readers do when they find these words in a book. "Great readers stop when they find an unknown word." I ask the students to repeat it out loud. Then I ask them to look at their turn and talk partners. Before we leave the mini-lesson, I have learners say the words, "I promise to stop when I find an unknown word because I am a great reader." Student giggle a bit, but make the promise. I continue, "Today, and every day, I want you to practice adding your collection by stopping and jotting any unknown words into your Vocabulary Journal."

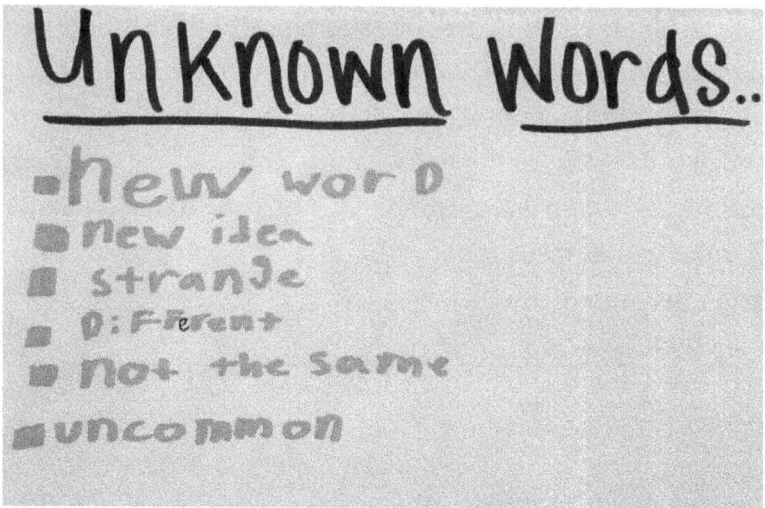

Figure 4.3 – Student brainstorm of unknown words

Repeated Words

Repeated and related words reappear and are echoed in one form or another throughout the text. So the next lesson focuses on these words. "Yesterday we talked about unknown words. Was it easy to find them?" Students share their successes, and we celebrate their ability to collect these important words. Students share a few of the words that they've found before I tell them about the final word type I want them to be able to collect on their own.

I have the anchor chart ready and the words repeated and connected are on the chart. "Why do you think these words are so important? Why would an author repeat a word or use a lot of words that are related?" They turn and talk with their partner before we share out as a group. The students offer ideas about what it means for words to be connected and why it might be important. This process is student driven to help build background knowledge, purpose, and motivation to do this challenging work.

After about 3 minutes, I have them come back together as a group and share out what they've decided. Some of the ideas that are shared are:

- They are important
- It has to do with the main idea
- They want us to focus on it
- They want you to remember it

I celebrate the thoughtful list of reasons an author would repeat or connect words, and I ask if I can add two reasons to the list. I write the words "mood" and "theme" on the anchor chart. I know that these words might be new for my ELLs and struggling learners, so I tell them not to be worried. While I give them a brief, working definition of what these terms mean, I remind them that I want them to focus their practice on finding repeated words that meet their criteria. I continue, "Today, and every day, I want you to practice adding your collections by stopping and jotting any repeated and connected words into your Vocabulary Journal." Students transition into independent reading, where they practice collecting these new types of words.

Teacher Choice Words:

Struggling students and ELLs generally have major gaps in the knowledge of even the 3,000 most frequently appearing words in the English language (Cameron, 2002). That is why they have sizeable vocabulary needs. Like student choice words, there are a number of words that teachers might find important for students to know. But it is impossible to teach students every word possible. That is why I've included 4 methods for selecting words and some functional language that might be helpful to consider when choosing which words should be taught, and which may not give you the most from the time you have to invest.

Essential Terms

Essential terms, or discipline-specific words, are words that students need to learn the material. Students cannot learn about cells if they don't know what a cell is. It is important to know that essential tier 3 words include all subjects (e.g. Science, Social Studies, Writing, Reading, Math, Art, etc.). But it also includes school specific words, hobbies, occupations, and more. Teachers should choose these words as the need arises. In other words, if it is a pre-requisite of learning for the day or for the unit, then it should be explicitly taught and reinforced with students.

Standards-based Words

Standards-based words are those that help students to understand the point of the learning experience. The common core state standards (CCSS) include language and vocabulary explicitly as part of the English Language Arts standards. But more important is that the CCSS weave vocabulary instruction throughout other standards, as well. Vocabulary instruction is referenced through conversations, reading, writing, speaking, listening, and the Math practices and standards, too. Because of this emphasis, taking the time to teach students the vocabulary words embedded in the CCSS only makes sense.

The standards also set the stage for what struggling students and ELLs can achieve when intentionally and specifically using language. This approach helps us as teachers see that we can use their strengths to develop their vocabularies and language in order to become better readers and more successful in school.

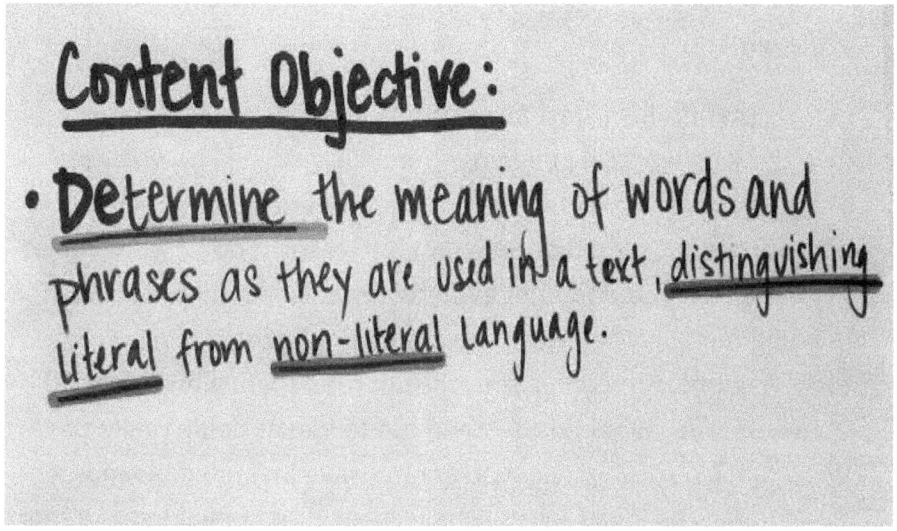

Figure 4.4 – Vocabulary of the standards

Thinking Words

Thinking words are the ones we associate with language objectives and the Depth of Knowledge Wheel (Webb, 2006). These are words like define, list, estimate, revise, and analyze that show how deeply students will need to think about and engage with a topic and what sort of language they will need to use in order to show that thinking. The problem is that these words are also subject to interpretation.

If I were to ask a room of 30 educators what it means to analyze a text, I'm sure I'd get 30 different working definitions of the word. It does not mean that any of those definitions are incorrect. It just means that the variance will lead to different products once people are expected to take action. Students are no different. They will also come to you with their interpretation of what these words mean. Or even worse, they will create a meaning for a word if none exists. This can have very serious consequences on the success of that learning task and overall achievement.

That is why I start any learning experience that contains new thinking words by building some background knowledge of that very word. I tell students, "Today, we are going to be practicing what we did during our mini-lesson. I don't want you to get nervous if you don't get everything perfectly right. We are still learning this together. But I do want you to take care in noticing the directions. Why don't you whisper read them while I read them out loud. What words stand out to you as being really important?" From that conversation, I have an incredible moment to reinforce the idea that they have ideas that are valued and that stopping and noticing words is valuable. It also creates a sense of safety when they know up front what it is that I am looking for in their thinking and in their answers.

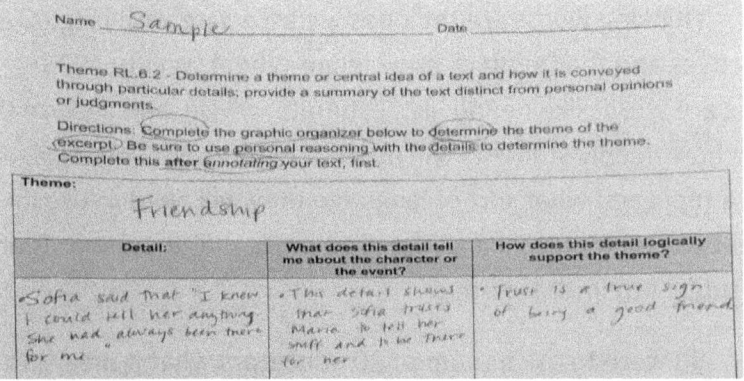

Figure 4.5 – Thinking words

Connected Words

Connected words are those that connect to the larger mood, theme, tone, or main idea developed by the author. These words help students to make powerful connections in their brains. They improve readers' ability to see that words are carefully chosen to achieve a certain end. These connections, then, become part of how teachers can build word consciousness and word banks at the same time.

For example, I explain that I am going to be talking about the Native American Discoveries in Social Studies. As part of the read aloud, which is at grade level, I know that my students will struggle with quite a number of words. But I know that my class does not need to know every word. I carefully pick out the following words: discovered, astonishment, and Gulf of St. Lawrence. Why these words? Simply put – these words help students to think about what the Native Americans felt as a result of the experience. In addition, each of these words is used more than once, meaning that perhaps the author wanted them to have a lasting impression.

But I don't tell them why I've chosen those words. Each time I go through this process I ask students to tell me what they think. "Why do you think these words are so important?" They turn and talk with their partners before we share out as a group. The students offer ideas as to how these words are connected and why they are important. This process gives students purpose and "buy in" as they later go to their journals to work on internalizing the word so that they can apply it and reference the word whenever they should need it.

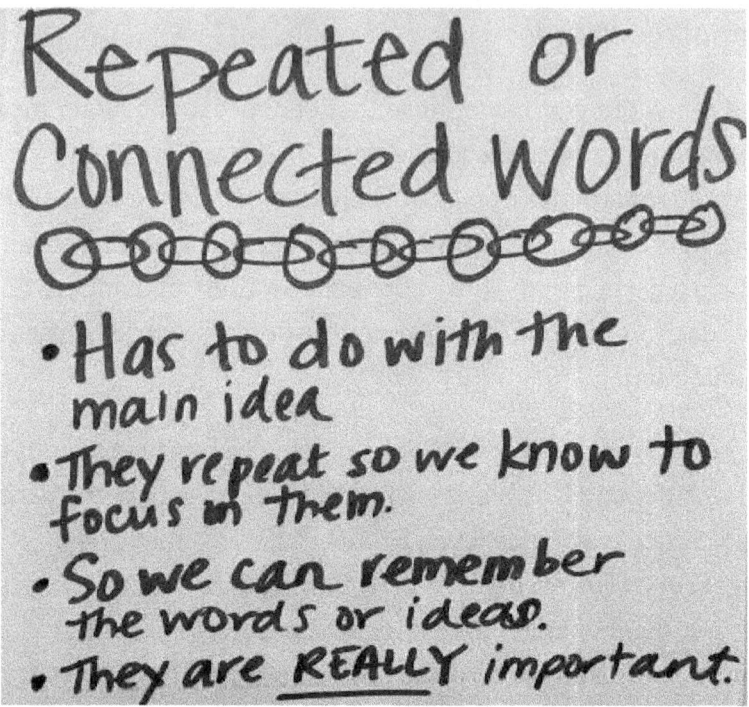

Figure 4.6 – Repeated or connected words anchor chart

    Whatever your preferred method of picking words is will work as long as it is consistent and students understand what the process means for them. If words are called essential words in August, it is helpful for students if they are still called the same thing in March.

    Once students have mastered this piece of the SPEED approach, they are well on their way to being able to work independently in their SPEED™ Vocabulary Journals. They have the word consciousness, the strategies to collect words, and the experience reading and engaging with a wide range of texts throughout the day. With these three elements and a well paired learning partner, students are able to work independently to organize their words and vocabulary development activities. This habit and independence, is possibly the most essential of the steps in their vocabulary acquisition journey.

CHAPTER 5
SPEED VOCABULARY WEEKLY LESSONS

The more real-world and relevant the lesson, activity, and/or resource, the more likely students are to engage and be willing to seek to comprehend on a deep level in reading and to invest their energies in revision and editing in their writing.

Regie Routman

The Vocabulary Journal Gradual Independence:

When students have learned the reasons for collecting words and how to collect them, they are ready to work individually or with a partner on the activities in their journal. These activities have been carefully selected to help students struggle with the word in a controlled setting so that then they are able to plan for, monitor, and apply the word outside of that vehicle. Working in the journal gives students the time to develop their understanding of the word using practical and research-based activities that are relevant and applicable to the real world.

Usually, students use their vocabulary journal (or word work) time to continue working on the words they have been collecting during Independent reading if they are focused on student choice words. Still, at other times, students are working with teacher choice words. Whether working with student choice words, teacher choice words, or a combination of the two, the vocabulary students work to develop, should be flexible and based on each individual's needs, the unit, and the structure of the class.

Each week, the journal adds one activity for students to practice using their unique set of words. For week 1 of the journal, students begin by pronouncing each word they've collected and approximating their words' meanings. Week by week, as students become comfortable using one strategy to learn the words, more activities are introduced. In the end, students have a range of up to 15 different research-based ways to develop their mastery of the vocabulary terms including:

- Word predictions
- Frayer modELLs
- Brainstorming examples and non-examples
- Writing authentic and memorable sentences
- Semantic analysis
- Shades of meaning
- Free choice games and activities
- Plan for using the words in the four domains of language
- Self-assessment of past word knowledge

Working with a partner or working independently:

Since the vocabulary journal is designed to support the words that meet the needs of each learner, it is possible for every student to have a unique set of words. Because of this, it is important to allow those students who prefer to work independently to have that flexibility.

There are times, however, when working with a partner is more ideal. Some of the benefits of working with a partner are as follows:

- Receive feedback around pronunciation
- Exposure to new strategies when approximating the words
- Exposure to double the vocabulary words leading to greater vocabulary acquisition
- Opportunity for meaningful dialogue that assist the learning process
- Someone to play games with

When picking partners, one of the many considerations for ELLs and struggling students is the reading level of the partnership and the L1 of the students. Students with similar reading levels tend to have better partnerships with their vocabulary journals because the vocabulary terms that they encounter tend to be around the same zone of proximal development. This is especially important if students are to begin absorbing their own words and incidentally, the words that their partner has collected.

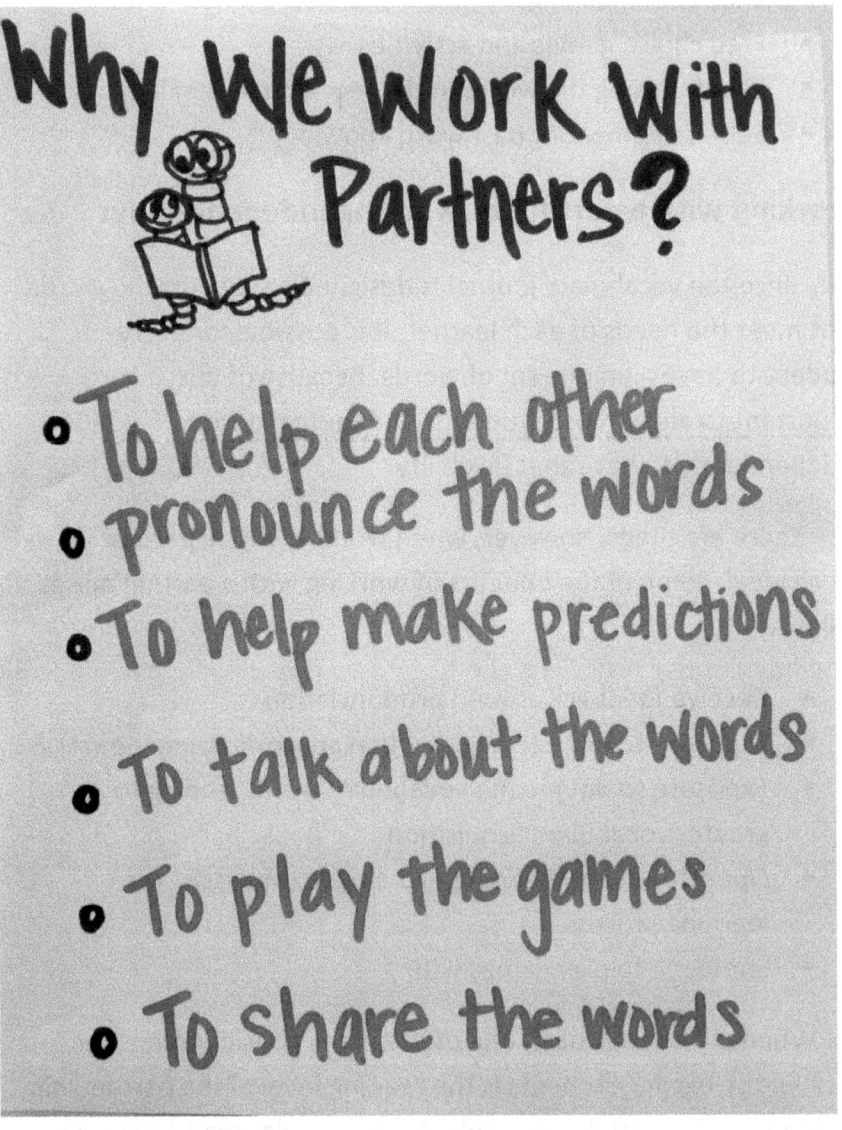

Figure 5.1 – Why we work with partners anchor chart

Word Predictions:

On week 1 we begin with the first activity – it is to predict the words' meanings. It helps students actively practice steps 1 in the SPEED™ system (Say the word and predict or approximate the word's meaning). We begin the week with the anchor lesson that provides the objective and hook for the activity.

On the first day, I tell students, "Today we are going to continue our journey as word collectors by focusing or paying attention to how we pronounce, or say, the new words, and predicting what the word means."

The class has already talked about what makes a word collectible, and we build on that knowledge by teaching the power of predicting a word's meaning. "When we come to a word that we do not know, what is the first thing we do?" I ask. I know that students understand that they need to stop as I hear the response being shared with turn and talk partners. It is the first step in awareness and the first step in building our vocabularies.

For students who are ELLs and struggling students, this concept of stopping first is one that I'll continue to go back to because it is critical to the success of the entire process and their overall achievement. This first step of saying and estimating the meaning of words might extend from 1-2 whole group lessons. But it will certainly be something that I return to during guided reading and one-on-one conferring.

"Today, when you are working in your vocabulary journals, I want you to remember the phrase: Stop, jot, predict. You are going to stop when you see an unknown word and say it out loud. You are going to jot your words down in your journal. And you are going to think about all the clues in the word, in the sentence, and in the book to try to come as close to what the word means as possible. Let me show you how."

During this first day it is important that I use the gradual release model (Pearson and Gallagher, 1983) in order to support the range of needs and build independence in my ELLs and struggling learners. As part of this gradual release I will explicitly teach the procedure that I want them to do. Then I will model how I use the procedure with a word while talking about my thought process (otherwise known as thinking aloud) during the model. After modeling the process, I will invite students to share the responsibility of thinking through another example. This "shared practice" is critical, as it gives my learners an opportunity to practice the activity and new strategy with me guiding them every step of the way. My students leave to practice the first activity independently with much more confidence after having seen it done and practicing with me.

This particular model with think aloud includes the following pieces:

- There are always clues about what the word means in the text
    - Sometimes the clues are in the word
    - Sometimes the clues are in the sentence
    - Sometimes the clues are in the paragraph
    - Sometimes the clues are on the page or in the book.
- Great readers check to see if their predictions makes sense by replacing the vocabulary word with the prediction or checking in our student dictionaries (Texas Center for Reading and Language Arts, 2002)

While I release students to practice their word pronunciations and predictions independently, I know that I will be there to work with students as they practice this new habit as it is developing. I have them practice it out loud and talk about why they chose that prediction, helping to pave the way for the explicit word learning strategies that will come. This practice, repetition, and questioning will repeat throughout the week as they work to become more independent with this part of the process.

Figure 5.2 – Predicting word meaning anchor chart

Frayer Model:

On week 2 we begin with the second activity – it is to work on Frayer models. It helps students actively practice steps 2 and 3 in the SPEED™ system (to create a picture or visual representation and to explain or describe the word). We begin this week with the anchor lesson that provides the objective and hook for the activity knowing that this strategy might take anywhere between 1-3 days for students to become more comfortable.

On this first day of vocabulary instruction, I tell students, "Today we are going to continue mastering vocabulary by focusing or paying attention to visuals and different ways to describe or explain the words."

Students hold a small copy of the graphic organizer while I start my model by going through each of the sections. "You each have a copy of what is called a Frayer Model. Do any of you notice anything important about this?" I give students a chance to turn and talk before having them share with the group. Some of the common responses are:

- There is a place to draw a picture
- You describe the word in your own way
- You add words that are like it
- You can put things that are opposite

"These are some amazing observations! One of the observations you shared was about drawing pictures. Do you notice how Mrs. Guilamo always uses pictures when we learn about new words and ideas?" I draw their attention to all the anchor charts around the room. These anchor charts are full of visual reminders and symbols that were carefully chosen to help learners remember the concepts they represent.

After talking about the reason I do this, I have students turn and talk about a picture or drawing they keep at home that helps them to remember a moment, event, or time in their lives. This connection to their lives helps build value for the activity and how it helps them as learners. It is also important for students to understand the logic behind the exercise. This metacognitive piece is what will allow them to become more independent as they continue with this practice over time.

"When is this the right strategy to use during word work?" I ask, knowing that the Frayer Model is one of many activities students might choose to master their words.

The Right Time to Use the Frayer Model:

- draw on prior knowledge to make connections among concepts.
- compare attributes and examples.
- think critically to find relationships between concepts and to develop deeper ones.
- develop understanding of key concepts and vocabulary.
- make visual connections and personal associations.
- review key vocabulary before a test or quiz.
- create a "vocabulary wall" for quick reference of word meanings.

Figure 5.3 – The right time to use the frayer model

Before students begin to work independently I use a common vocabulary word from a previous unit – one that all my students are familiar with. I model the process using the graphic organizer with the class. I think aloud about the type and quality of answers that will impact their acquisition of the term. I then have them practice with their turn and talk partner before releasing students to practice their Frayer Models independently.

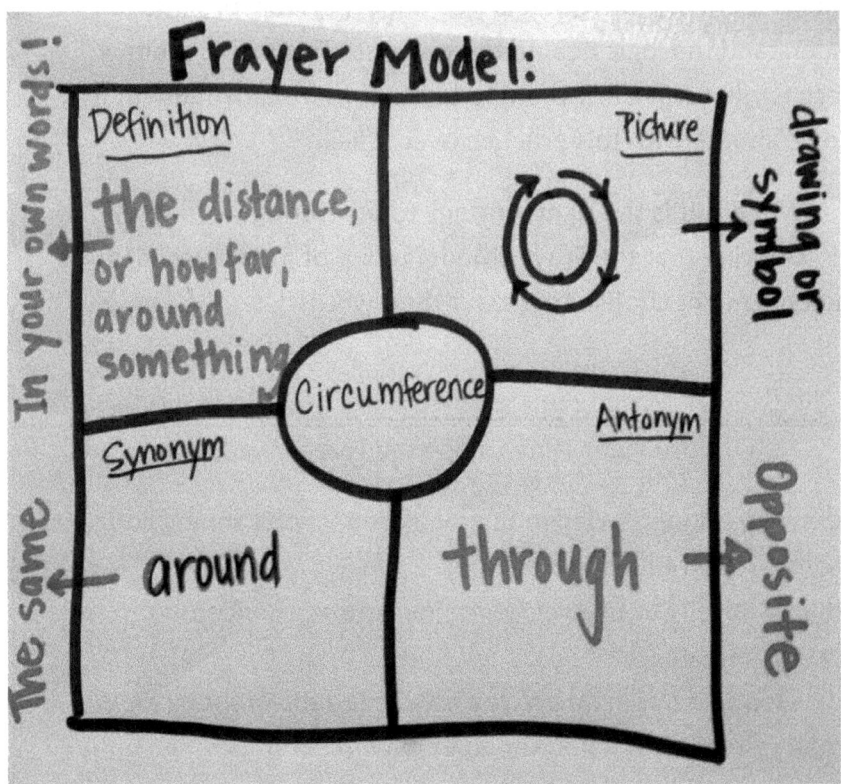

Figure 5.4 – Frayer model example from model lesson

After the shared practice, I ask students to share their responses (visuals, definitions, synonyms, and antonyms) with the group. "How does that picture help you to remember or think about that word?" I ask the group. This is a question that allows them to discuss the value and intentionality of their work. The intentionality behind their practice will have huge benefits in the long run for their independence and vocabulary expansion.

Brainstorming Examples and Non-examples:

On week 3 we being with the third activity – it is to work on examples and non-examples and an extension of the Frayer Model from the previous week. It helps students actively practice steps 3 and 4 in the SPEED™ system (to explain or describe the word and engage in varied and extended practice). Again, we begin this week with the anchor lesson that provides the objective and hook for the activity. Because students have been working with Frayer ModELLs, this lesson usually only takes one day for students to develop into confident practitioners of the strategy.

On the first day of rolling out the strategy or activity, I tell students, "Today we are going to deepen our knowledge of these vocabulary words by focusing or paying attention to examples and non-examples. Before I model this activity for you, I think it is important that we all have the same understanding of what an example is. Turn and talk to your partner about what it means to give an example.

I listen to student conversations about what they think the word means. I can hear many learners using the sentence frame I've posted, "I think an example is..." These sentence starters accompany most anchor lessons. It is a critical scaffold for my ELLs and struggling students so that I am scaffolding the amount of language they need to formulate on their own. I want them to really think about this word, and so I help remove the other challenges they might have in formalizing their thinking. When I ask them to share out, some of the common answers are:

- Model

- One kind
- A sample of something
- One way to use the word

We go through each of the responses, one by one, helping students to see why these are powerful descriptions of the word. I then tell students, "Examples help us to generalize. That's a juicy word! To generalize means to think about what is the most simple meaning of the word so that you can apply it other ways of using the word. And that is what I want us to practice today. I want you to watch me as I model making a generalization about my word."

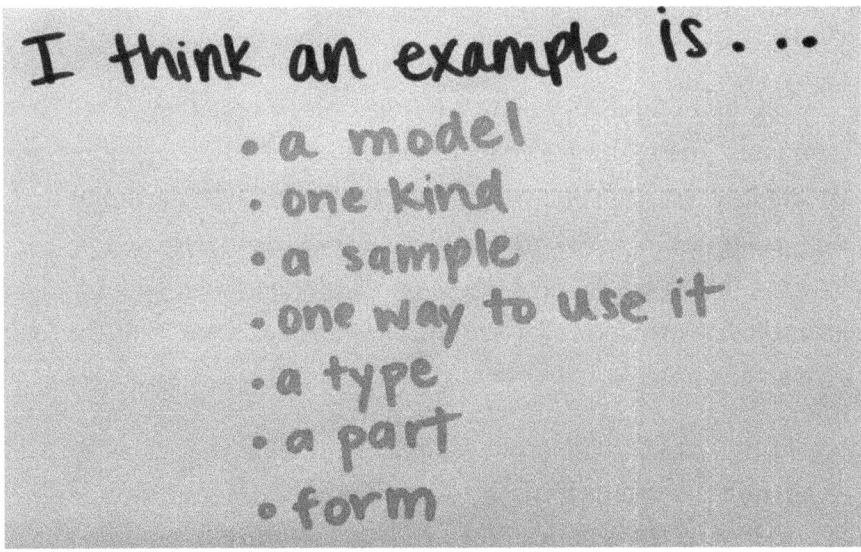

Figure 5.5 –Example brainstorm from model lesson

I model a T-chart with examples on the left side and non-examples on the right side. I pull out the book I read to students during the previous day's read aloud. Since they just heard the story the day before, it is still fresh in their memories. "Watch as I use this chart to think of examples and non-examples of this word." Again, it is important that my learners know what makes a good example of what this activity looks like and sounds like before beginning a shared or independent practice.

After this model, shared practice, and discussion, students head to their vocabulary journals to practice. While they might practice other activities that we've already tried together later in the week, it is essential that students practice this particular activity right away. They will need to apply their learning while it is fresh in their minds, and they will need my support, and I move throughout the room supporting partnerships at work. This activity is especially challenging because it encourages students to start appreciating the underlying concepts and nuances of the word in a more reflective way than the previous and more superficial expectations. However, its strong impact on lasting mastery and application of the words makes it invaluable to students' success.

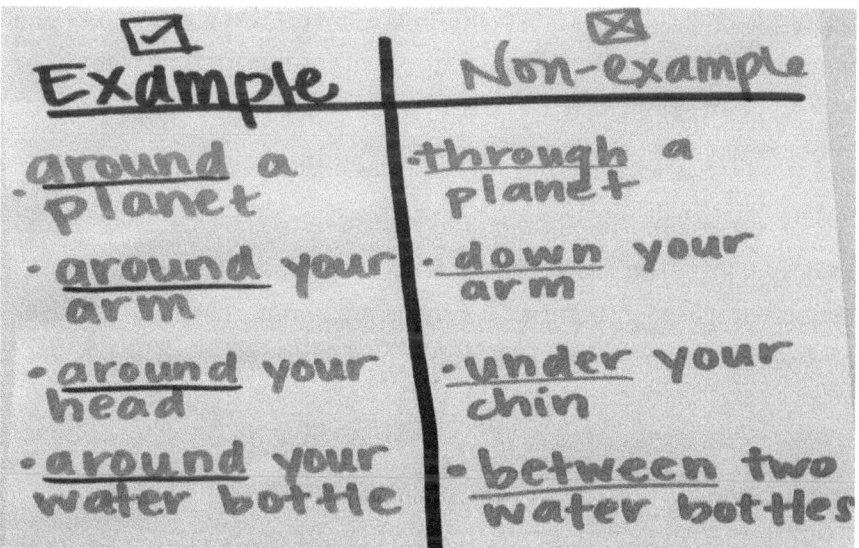

Figure 5.6 – Example/Nonexample sample from model lesson

Writing Authentic and Memorable Sentences:

On week 4 we begin with the fourth activity – which is to work on categorizing and original sentences. It helps students actively practice steps 4 and 5 in the SPEED™ system (to engage in varied and extended practice and to discuss the meaning of the words). On the first day of rolling out this activity, I start the anchor lesson with the question, "How many of us have written or read a one-word story?"

Students start to giggle and look around to see if this is a real question. As I look at them with a blank face, the giggles turn to looks of musing and consideration. One student mentions a book with no words. Several students mention books with only a few words on each page. They continue to consider the question.

"Let me ask you this. Can we communicate well, using only one word? And do stories need to have more than one word?" Before I can tell them to explain their answers, they've already begun arguing why it can't be a story without more than one word. "I can speak or write, but (I) need more words for people to know how you mean them," says one of my newcomers.

I thank her for sharing and reinforce to the class that she is exactly right. After restating the answer modeling the use of rich language, we brainstorm why it might be beneficial to use our new words in sentences and what type of sentences are the best.

Why we write sentences	What makes a good practice sentence
• Improve my writing • Get to see if I can use the word correctly • Use my learning from the other days • Practice using the word to learn it better • See words that are connected • Help show what the word means	• **Sentences that use connected word pairs or groups** • **A sentence that could be in the story we read** • **Original** • **Memorable** • **Sentences that have analogies or examples in them** • **Riddles that can be used during free choice with your partner**

Figure 5.7 – How and why we write original sentences

After the brainstorm, we use a word from our Science unit to model and think aloud. We share the responsibility of checking our sentence against our anchor chart. I then give students another word from our math unit to practice with a partner. Again, giving them terms with which they are familiar is important so that they can practice the new activity without the barriers of other challenges they may face. As students are creating these original sentences with their turn and talk partner, it is important that I circulate the room to problem-solve with students as they practice.

Once we have had time to share out, we go into independent practice. Students know that although it might not be the first activity in their journal, that it is very important to begin that practice right away. I tell them, "So today, as you work in your vocabulary journals, what should you do?"

"Practice while it's fresh," I hear. Before I send them off, I have them tell their turn and talk partners what their sentences will look like using the anchor chart we've created together. This step is important for a number of reasons. English learners and struggling students struggle with multi-step directions and have increased outcomes when able to articulate what each step in the process looks like before having to implement it. Additionally, this helps to make the key goals of the learning concrete in the brain so that the benefit is realized.

Figure 5.8 – Practice anchor chart from model lesson

Semantic Feature Analysis:

On week 5 we begin with the fifth activity – which is to work on creating a semantic feature analysis grid. Semantic feature analyses help students actively practice steps 4 and 5 in the SPEED™ system (to engage in varied and extended practice and to discuss the meaning of the words). To roll out this activity, I start the anchor lesson with the question, "Do ALL words have clues about their meanings? Turn and talk to your partner."

I have a blank anchor chart ready, but today I choose not to write anything in preparation. This concept is very challenging for all students – even native language speakers and avid readers. But I know that once they get the hang of this, my English learners and struggling students will become masters of using this strategy because it requires less background knowledge.

"Let's finish our sentence in 5," I begin before counting down slowly. "So what do you think?"

The answers are as I expected. Yes, no, and sometimes. I urge them to talk more about why they have those opinions and to give examples of how all words do or how some words might not. They struggle, but it is a healthy struggle. I monitor to see the level of frustration on my learners. I know that this frustration level cannot exceed a certain point or my learners will shut down and I will have to spend weeks rebuilding their confidences – which is the heart of ELLs' and struggling students' willingness to take chances with language, literacy, and learning in general.

"What if I told you that ALL words do have clues (I smile), what is one type of clue you might look for? Write that one clue in the air with your finger," I add. I have students write their answers in the air so that I can see that every learner is engaged in the practice and that we are engaging multiple senses. I also limit it to one clue because I want to make sure that they feel safe after the struggle they just faced. It is one of the ways that I balance the experience to always keep them in the zone of proximal development.

"Do I have one brave scholar who would like to share?" I ask. I am sure to celebrate the contribution, the bravery, and the way they are working to make meaning.

"The trick is that there are clues everywhere if we know where and how to look. When we look at a word, we can look at all of its qualities or characteristics to get more information about what the word means. And from the different parts of the word, I can learn more about what it means. Watch me, as I take a look at the word *teacher*."

I start underlining and circling different parts of the word in various colors. Teacher has two syllables, it has a suffix (-er), it has two vowELLs together (-ea-), it is a noun, it starts with a t. I list all of these features on the graphic organizer that mirrors what they have in their journal. "Look at all these clues and parts of the word that can help me figure out the meaning or find connections between other words," I share.

I write the word teacher in the first cell of row one and proceed to check off each of the features. "Can someone think of another word that we've been using in Science that we can add to this chart?" Students add the word *sediment*. Together we look to see if that word contains the same features as the word teacher. One by one, we write an "x" in each cell for the features the word has. I then have them pick another word to practice with their turn and talk partner before sharing out.

"Today, I want you to practice using your semantic feature analysis. And whenever you are working with teacher choice words from Math, Science, and Social Studies, I want you to consider using this as one of your core strategies," I tell them. I include this request because I know that many of the tier 3 words that they'll encounter will have similar word parts, paving the way for the word learning strategies they'll be developing.

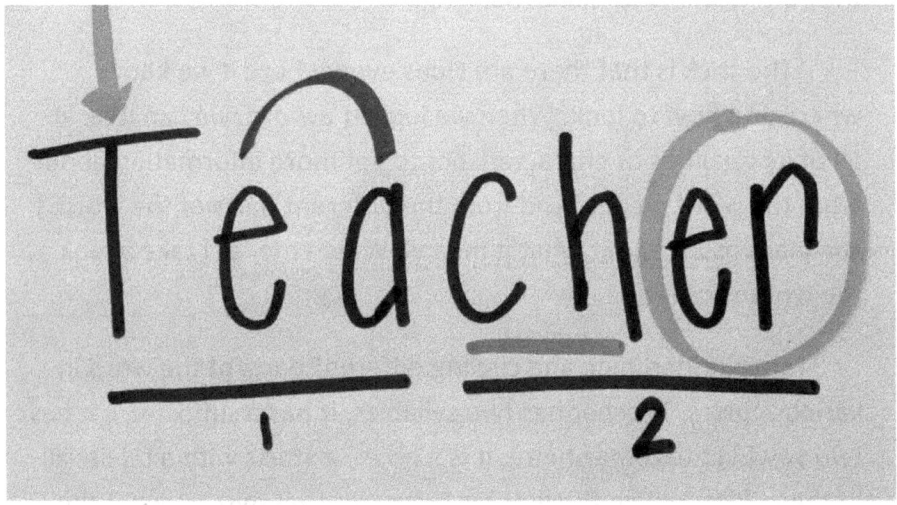

Figure 5.9 – Semantic feature analysis example from model lesson

What things do you notice about this list of words? Are the words all verbs, do the words all have prefixes, is there a spelling pattern, etc.? Write your words on the left. Write the properties of the words at the top. Write an "x" in each square to show which words have which properties.

Academic Vocabulary	Feature/ Property	Noun	Suffix	2 syllables	Starts with	has a blend
Teacher		✓	✓	✓	✓	✓
Sediment		✓	✓	NO	No	No

Figure 5.10 – Semantic feature analysis example from model lesson

Shades of Meaning or Semantic Gradients:

On week 6 we begin with the sixth and final structured activity – which is to develop a semantic gradient. Semantic gradients help students extend their understanding of a word by connecting them to related words that have similar but small differences in their meaning. This ultimately leads them to expanding their vocabularies even more by highlighting the importance of precise language and the impact that small differences can make. Doing semantic gradients helps students actively practice steps 4 and 5 in the SPEED™ system (to engage in varied and extended practice and to discuss the meaning of the words). To roll out this activity, I start the anchor lesson by having students describe the graphic that I've drawn on the anchor chart.

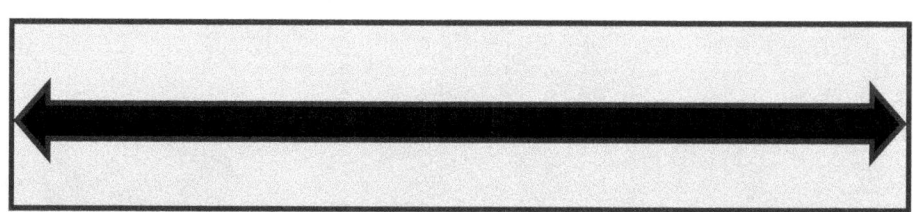

After students share out, I consolidate their answers and work to give them a student-friendly definition of semantic gradient. "Semantic gradients are when we create ranges of words that show the small differences in their meanings." Students repeat the definition to their turn and talk partner then begin to discuss why they would want to make a semantic gradient. I thank them for the level of thinking. Since not all students will arrive at the idea that it helps them to expand their vocabularies by studying similar but related words, I usually tell them this benefit. We then begin talking through the process of creating a gradient using an example word. "To start my semantic gradient, I put my vocabulary word in the middle, then the strongest synonym on one end, and next I put the strongest antonym on the other end. Now, I start to fill in the 'shades of meaning' with other related words that that fit along that scale."

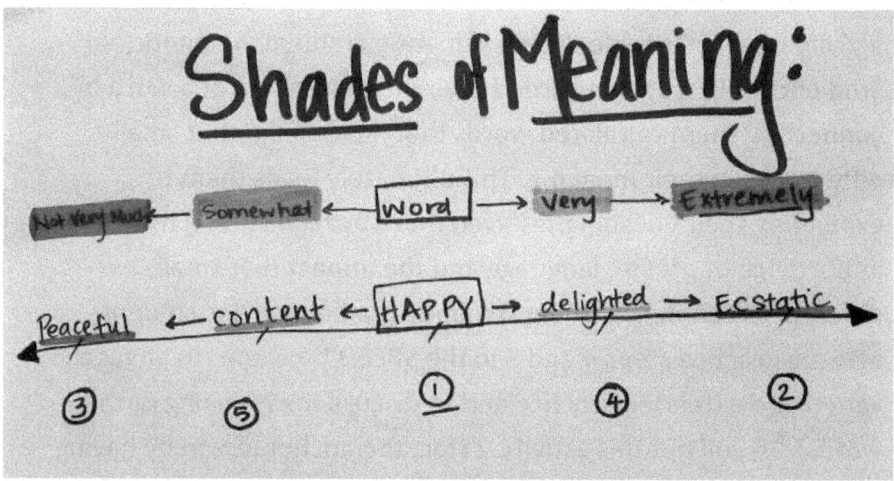

Figure 5.11 – Shades of meaning example from model lesson with supports

For our shared practice, I put the word *sad* in the middle of the gradient. Then I ask students, "Where to next? What is the next word I should try to place?" I am looking for them to direct me to either end of the gradient. However, I know this practice is new, and I am prepared to shift my role in the practice if needed.

Another scaffold that I have used successfully with students is to label the steps in the process on the model problem as seen below. This is just one of many ways that I can help frame students' thinking so that they are able to build the routine independently.

"Turn and talk to your partner about what additional words you would add to this gradient to complete the continuum." As we work through the *sad*, I continue to ask student partners to explain their word choices. "Why?" I say as I listen in to the turn and talk partners. On this occasion a student disagrees with their partner.

"I don't think this word goes here," she admits.

"Why not?" I probe.

"Well, I think that miserable is more sad than depressed."

"Why?" I question again with a smile.

"I don't know, it just is," she confesses.

I ask the pair, "Okay, can you think of an example of a time that you or someone you knew was miserable? How did it feel? What about depressed? I want you to talk about those examples and decide together where it should go on the continuum."

I bring the students back to whole group. We finish the gradient together on the anchor chart. I then ask students to share some of the other words they generated in their partnerships. "I'm passing out a card to each of you with words that related to sad. You job is to get in order according to its shade of meaning. I want sad in the middle. Now, without using any words, organize yourselves with the strongest synonyms to the right and the strongest antonyms to the left. Go."

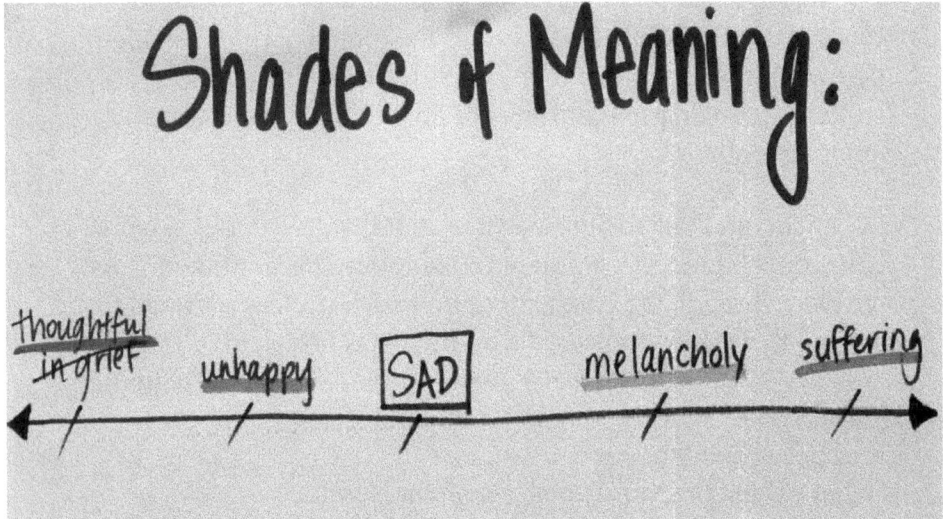

Figure 5.13 – Shades of meaning shared practice lesson

After about 3 minutes, I have the class talk about their choices. "There are some words that I might change in this line. Is there anyone who sees a word that they might change?" I ask. Then I probe "Why?" It is part B to every question. Students know it is coming, and that it is the thinking behind the answer that I'm looking for. It is this profound thinking about how they arrived at their opinions that continues to prove to be worth it. For some students, describing how they know what they know is tricky because of their limited English. In these situations, we work to native language buddies, nonlinguistic representations, and technology (translation headsets, software programs, etc.) to help bridge their ideas from their L1 to English.

"Today, I want you to practice using your shades of meaning page. And whenever you are working with student choice words from fictional texts, I want you to consider using this as one of your core strategies," I tell them. I include this request because I know that many of them will expand their tier 1 and 2 vocabulary bases through this practice. This will have huge payoffs in their reading and writing development over time.

Free Choice Games and Activities:

On this last day of rolling out vocabulary activities, we talk about continuing to develop their vocabulary growth through free choice activities. "So, what is a free choice?" I ask them.

While students are used to having a choice and say in what happens in class, they look doubtfully at the simplicity of the question. "We are free to choose whatever we want," says Samuel.

"That is exactly right," I tell them. "Over the last few weeks, I have given you teacher choice activities that have been studied and proven to work. These activities are other people's ideas. But you all are brilliant scholars; you have proven that to me each and every day this year. You have plenty of ideas of games you can play and activities you can do to help you learn the words, don't you?" I challenge.

We roll out this final phase of the approach with a simple brainstorm. "What are some games and activities that you think might help you learn your words?" I turn over to the group. Students are eager to share their ideas, and I write them down as fast as I can. As each student shares their idea, I have them give a single-sentence summary of what the game is for the group. This helps me to understand the connection and give others in the class a brief overview in case they have not heard of it either.

"In your appendix of your journal, you have several ideas of things you can do for free choice. But remember, the choice is for you and your partner to make. If you want to choose one of the activities from the appendix, one from this list, or one of your own making, the choice is yours to make. The only rule is that it must help you do what?" I test.

"Help us learn the words," the class shares out.

"That's right. It must help you learn the words," I repeat. Then I write those words on the anchor chart and underline it in order to make it stand out.

"Today, I want you to practice using a free choice activity to help you deepen your knowledge of your words. You might find that over the next few months, you might want to use free choice activities with all of your words. That's perfectly fine. When you do work on free choice activities, I want you to make sure think about three questions. Why is that activity the best one to help you learn the words? Is there any part of the game that you need to change in order to make it work for the words you are studying? And is there another game that would be better for you to play for this kind of words next time?"

I share these three questions with students now because the metacognitive awareness will help them to take control over their learning (Kuhn, 2000), allowing students to be more independent and flexible with their learning. This awareness may be limited in the initial weeks of practice. But the next few months of intense coaching on comprehension and word learning strategies will help to develop their mastery of this skill.

Academic Vocabulary with SPEED

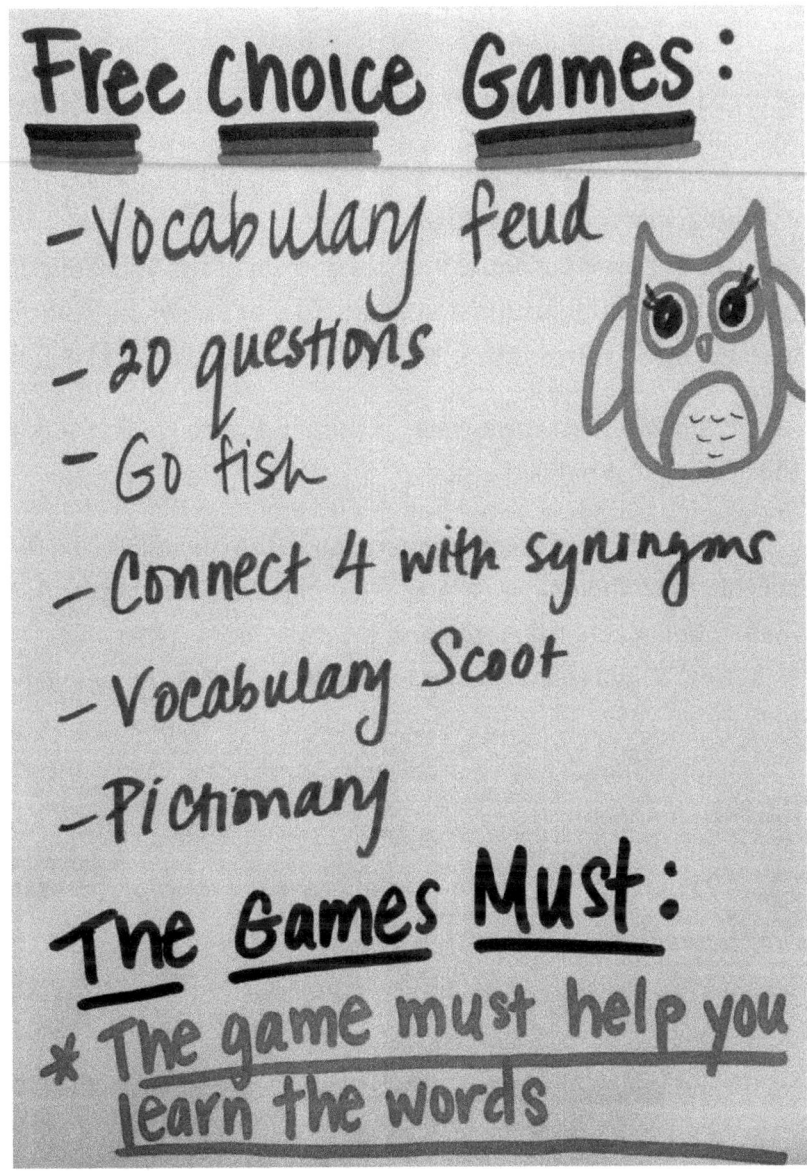

Figure 5.14 – Free choice game brainstorm from model lesson

Plan for Using Words in the Four Domains of Language:

As part of every week in the SPEED™ approach to vocabulary instruction, students actively plan for how they are going to use their vocabulary words outside of the vocabulary journal time. Students must understand that the whole point of learning these words is to use them in their daily use of language.

My question to students is this: "Why are we learning all these words? What is the point?"

Students are eager to share, and I call on individuals to contribute to the dialogue. Answers range from helping students read to being able to understand what students are saying. "Precisely," I tell them. "What I am hearing is that the whole point of learning all these words is to be able to use them and understand them." I write the words, "I WILL USE MY WORDS" on the anchor chart.

"How can we use these words?" I ask the class. Some of the answers I get are the following:

- In our writing
- On our homework
- When we are playing our games
- During writing class

"These are great ideas of how to use the words. And what I am hearing in all of your answers is that you can use these words when working on any reading, writing, listening, and speaking activity," I beam. "You can use these words when using language every day. These words are juicy words; they are words that make you rich with knowledge. I want you to practice getting rich with words—a lot!" I laugh.

The students laugh, but I continue. "Keep track of how rich you are getting with words in your journals. Be honest with yourselves when marking the different ways you used the words so that we can celebrate your focus and word wealth as your vocabularies grow!"

"Today, and every day, I want you to practice monitoring how well you are using your rich words in school and in life outside of your vocabulary journal time. On Fridays, I also want you to take some time to reflect on how well you remember your words from the previous week. It should only take a few minutes, but it is very important for you to know if all your work has paid off. This self-reflection helps to anchor all vocabulary words (both student and teacher choice). It also puts the ownership of learning the words into the hands of my students. This puts them in the driver seat of their learning – they are in control. When they see huge growth in their reading and writing development, students can own that success along with the strategies and tools they employed to get there.

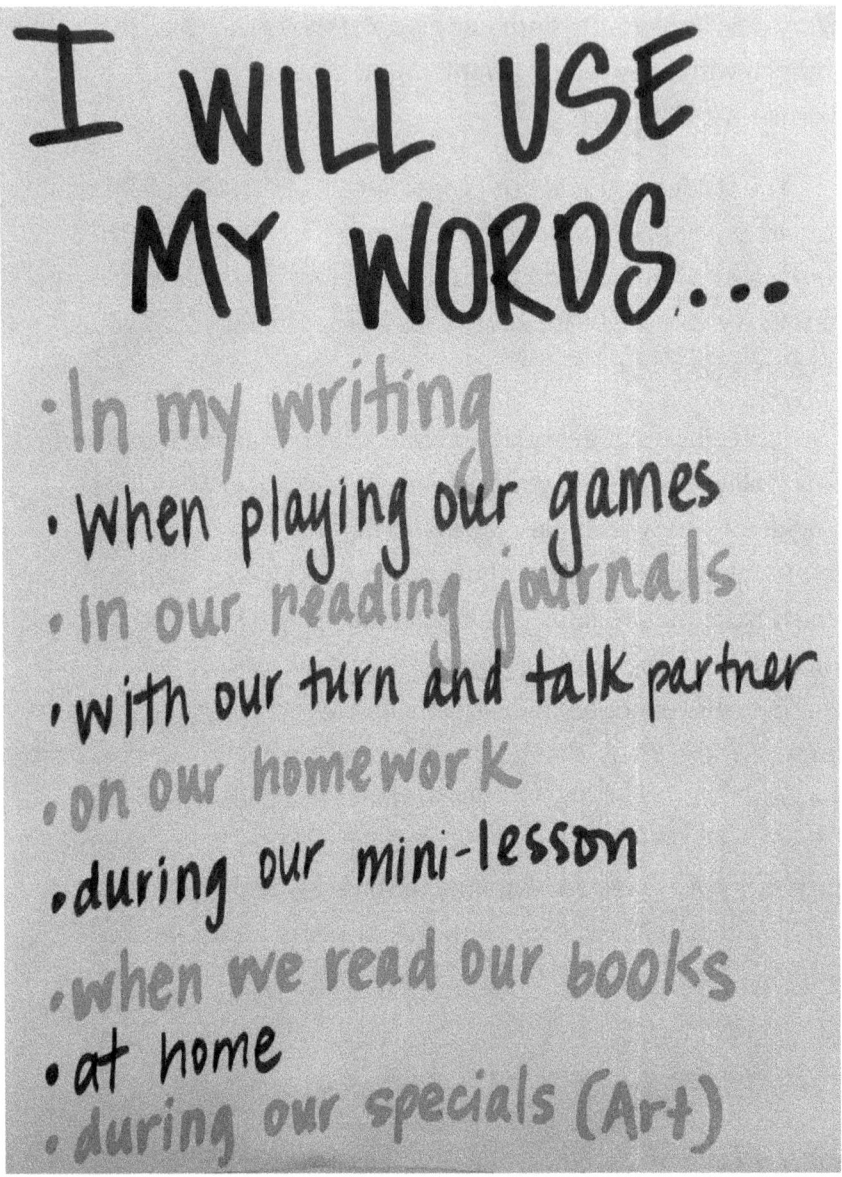

Figure 5.15 – Ways we use our words anchor chart model lesson

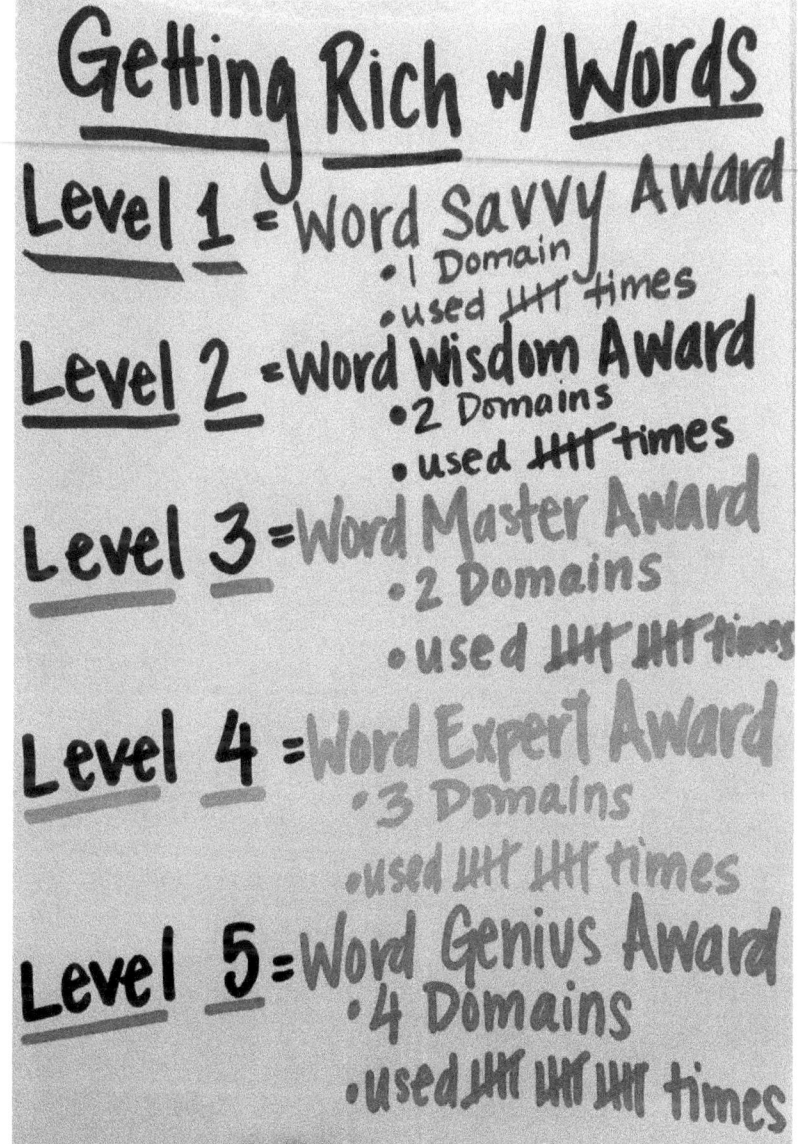

Figure 5.15 – Getting rich with words achievement levels anchor chart

APPENDIX I
The First 45 Days

1	2	3	4	5	6	7
8	9	10	11	12	13	14
15	16	17	18	19	20	21
22	23	24	25	26	27	28

Academic Vocabulary with SPEED

Day 1	Mini-Lesson Teach Point	Critical Question	Keeping It Fresh – Independent Practice	Reference
WEEK 1 Day 1	Notice words around you Language objectives	How does my environment promote language experiences?	Students tour the room and resources – classroom library and student dictionaries	See page 18
Day 2	Our words matter	Do words matter?	Free write – why my name matters to me	See page 17
Day 3	5 Finger Rule	What is the 5 Finger Rule?	Students pick out books from the classroom library for book bins	See page 20
Day 4	My job during independent reading	Do I have a job to do during independent	Practice independent reading	See page 20

		reading?		
Day 5	What great readers do when they read independently	What can I do to show that I am a great reader?	"Kid watch" while students independently read	See page 41
WEEK 2 Day 6	Review and building stamina Student choice words	Where will you find the words to grow my vocabulary?	Try to reach 7 minutes of reading stamina	See page 39
Day 7	Read *Max's Words* - What makes a word collectible?	What are juicy words?	Try to find 3 juicy words – add these words to your journal	See page 39
Day 8	Unknown words	What does unknown mean?	Stop and jot unknown words – add them to your journal	See page 40
Day 9	Connected words	Why might repeated words be	Try to identify 1 word that repeats in your	See page 44

		important?	independent reading book – add it to your journal	
Day 10	Challenging Talk Sentence starters	Why will we talk so much about our work?	Accountable talk – share the words you collected this week and why.	See page 25
WEEK 3 Day 11	Teacher helps the class brainstorm why we work with partners Begin partnered vocabulary development	How can I grow faster if I work with a partner?	Share your words with your new word learning partner?	See page 47
Day 12	Predictions – what are context clues	How can we make better predictions?	Look at the words around the unknown word when making your predictions	See page 29/30

Day 13	Predictions – what are morphemic word clues	How can we make better predictions?	Look at all of the parts of the unknown word when making your predictions	See page 29
Day 14	Teacher helps brainstorm how and when we can use our words	Why learn all these words?	Practice using at least one word in Reading, Writing, Speaking, and Listening	See page 65
Day 15	Teacher modeling - setting a goal and Self Reflection Why we learn words - PROMISE	Do I remember the words I've learned?	Plan, use, and monitoring how you apply your knowledge of words outside of vocabulary time.	See Page 65/66
WEEK 4 Day	The purpose of a read aloud and text from other	Can words make me rich?	Trading modest words for rich ones	See page 24 and page 21

16	classes 3 Tier of Words			
Day 17	Teacher Choice words Essential terms – Science lesson Connected words – Science lesson	What are the words that are needed to be successful in this lesson?	Add the teacher choice words to your journal Underline your CCSS on your class activity	See page 42
Day 18	CCSS – Math lesson Thinking words – Math lesson	How do these words change the level of difficulty of this activity?	Read the directions on your practice page, circle the CCSS and thinking words. Add these words to your journal.	See page 43
Day 19	Frayer Model – teacher modeling	What do you notice about this graphic?	Practice in vocabulary journal	See page 51

Day 20	Right Time – class brainstorm	When is the best time to use the Frayer model?	Practice in vocabulary journal	See page 52
WEEK 5 Day 21	Brainstorm of Example/Non-example Teacher explains "generalizing" and modELLs using the Example/non-example T-chart with sentence starter	What makes a good example?	Practice in vocabulary journal	See page 53
Day 22	Model another Example/non-example T-chart without sentence starter Conferring with students	When is the right time to use this word?	Practice in vocabulary journal	See page 53

Day 23	Conferring with students	What is the one strategy that can make me a better and more mindful reader?	Practice in vocabulary journal	See page 52/53
Day 24	Conferring with students	What is the one strategy that can make me a better and more mindful reader?	Practice in vocabulary journal	See page 52/53
Day 25	Conferring with students	What is the one strategy that can make me a better and more mindful reader?	Practice in vocabulary journal	See page 52/53
WEEK 6 Day 26	Brainstorm "what makes a good and authentic sentence?" Model creating authentic	Can we communicate well using only 1 word?	Practice in vocabulary journal	See page 55

		sentences		
Day 27	Keep it Fresh	Is this a book-worthy sentence?	Practice in vocabulary journal	See page 55/56
Day 28	Guided Reading	What is the one strategy that can make me a better and more mindful reader?	Practice in vocabulary journal	See page and Strategy cards
Day 29	Guided Reading	What is the one strategy that can make me a better and more mindful reader?	Practice in vocabulary journal	See page 22/23 and Strategy cards
Day 30	Guided Reading	What is the one strategy that can make me a better and more mindful	Practice in vocabulary journal	See page 22/23 and Strategy cards

		reader?		
WEEK 7 Day 31	Semantic word analysis model with the word *teacher*	Do all words have clues?	Try adding the semantic word analysis this week. Begin with 2 words.	See page 58
Day 32	Word Clues	What clues do words have?	Practice in vocabulary journal	See page 23
Day 33	Guided Reading	What is the one strategy that can make me a better and more mindful reader?	Practice in vocabulary journal	See page 22/23 and Strategy cards
Day 34	Guided Reading	What is the one strategy that can make me a better and more mindful reader?	Practice in vocabulary journal	See page 22/23 and Strategy cards
Day 35	Guided Reading	What is the one strategy that can	Practice in vocabulary	See page 22/23 and Strategy

		make me a better and more mindful reader?	journal	cards
WEEK 8 Day 36	Shades of meaning – student describe the gradient line. Teacher modELLs gradient with the word happy	Why make a word gradient?	Students practice gradient with the word sad.	See page 61/62
Day 37	Review shades of meaning. Students line up into a gradient with cards	How can I tell if words have a stronger meaning?	Practice gradients with fictional text in vocabulary journal	See page 62 and Strategy cards
Day 38	Guided Reading	What is the one strategy that can make me a better and more mindful reader?	Practice in vocabulary journal	See page 22/23 and Strategy cards

Day 39	Guided Reading	What is the one strategy that can make me a better and more mindful reader?	Practice in vocabulary journal	See page 22/23 and Strategy cards
Day 40	Guided Reading	What is the one strategy that can make me a better and more mindful reader?	Practice in vocabulary journal	See page 22/23 and Strategy cards
WEEK 9 Day 41	Teacher explains free choice agreements	What is free choice?	Practice in vocabulary journal	See page 63
Day 42	Concept mapping	Are there any other choices?	Practice in vocabulary journal	See page 27
Day 43	Using cognates	Is there a way to learn even more words?	Practice in vocabulary journal	See page 29

Day 44	Review free choice and encourage a new game	What can I play today to help me in my journey?	Practice in vocabulary journal	-
Day 45	Review all the vocabulary activities – balancing all the pieces.	What does it mean to be balanced in our work?	Discuss balance during one on one conference	-

APPENDIX II
BIBLIOGRAPHY

Allington, R. (2001). *What really matters for struggling readers: Designing research-based programs*. New York: Longman.

Alvermann, D. & Phelps, S. (2002). *Content reading and literacy: Succeeding in today's diverse classrooms*. Boston: Allyn and Bacon.

Anderson, R. C., & Nagy, W. (1991). Word meanings. In R. Barr, M. Kamil, P. Mosenthal, & P. D. Pearson (Eds.), Handbook of reading research (Vol. II). New York: Longman.

Anderson, R. C., (1996). Research foundations to support wide reading. In V. Greaney (Ed.), *Promoting reading in developing countries* (pp. 55-77). New York: International Reading Association.

August, D., (2009). Developing literacy in Spanish-speaking children: Acquisition of vocabulary in English (Technical Report 1 Submitted to the National Institute of Child Health and Human Development). Washington, DC: Center for Applied Linguistics.

August, D., & Shanahan, T. (2006). *Developing literacy in second-language learners: Report of the National Literacy Panel on language-minority children and youth*. Mahwah, NJ: Erlbaum.

August, D., * Snow, C. (2007). Developing vocabulary in English-langauge learners: A review of the experimental research. In B. M. Taylor & J. E. Ysseldyke (Eds.), *Effective instruction for struggling readers, K-6* (pp. 84-105). New York: Teachers College Press.

Baumann, J. F., Blachowicz, C. L. Z., Manyak, P. C., Graves, M. F., & Olejnik, S. (2009) *Development of a multi-faceted, comprehensive, vocabulary instructional program for the upper-elementary grades*. Washington, DC: U.S. Department of Education, Institute of Education Sciences, National Center for Education Research.

Baumann, J. F., Edwards, E. C., Boland, E., Olejnik, S., & Kame"enui, E. J. (2003). Vocabulary tricks: Effects of instruction in morphology and context on fifth-grade students' ability to derive and infer word meaning. *American Educational Research Journal.*

Beck, I. L., & McKeown, M. G. (1991). Conditions of vocabulary acquisition. In P. D. Pearson (Ed.), *The handbook of reading research, vol. 2* (pp. 789-814). New York: Longman.

Beck, I. L., & McKeown, M. G. (2004). Direct and rich vocabulary instruction. In J. F. Baumann &E. J. Kame'enui (Eds.), *Vocabulary instruction* (pp. 13-27). New York: Guilford.

Beck, I. L., McKeown, M. G., & Kucan, L. (2002). *Bringing words to life: Robust vocabulary instruction.* New York: Guildford.

Beck, I. L., McKeown, M. G., & Kucan, L. (2008). Creating robust vocabulary: Frequently asked questions and extended examples. New York: Guilford Press.

Biemiller, A. (2004). Teaching vocabulary in the primary grades: Vocabulary instruction needed. In J. F. Baumann & E. J. Kame'enui (Eds.), *Vocabulary instruction: Research to practice* (pp. 28-40). New York: Guildford.

Blachowicz, C. L. Z., & Fisher, P. (2010). *Teaching vocabulary in all classrooms* (4th ed.). Englewood Cliffs, NJ: Merrill/Prentice Hall.

Bravo, M. A., Hiebert, E. H., & Pearson, P. D. (2007). Tapping the linguistic resources of Spanish/English bilinguals: The role of cognates in science. In R. K. Wagner, A. Muse, & K. Tannenbaum (Eds.), *Vocabulary development and its implications for reading comprehension* (pp. 140-156). New York: Guilford.

Buikema, J. L., & Graves, M. F. (1998=3). *Teaching students to use context cues to infer word meanings.* Journal of Reading, 36, 450-457.

Calderón, M., August, D., Slavin, R., Durán, D., Madden, N., & Cheung, A. (2005). Bringing words to life in classrooms with English language learners. In E. H. Hiebert & M. L. Kamil (Eds.), Teaching and learning vocabulary: Bringing research to practice. Mahwah, NJ: Erlbaum.

Carlo, M., August, D., McLaughlin, B., Snow, C., Dressler, C., Lippman, D., et al. (2004). Closing the gap: Addressing the vocabulary needs of English-language learners in bilingual and mainstream classrooms. *Reading Research Quarterly*, 38, 188-215.

Carlo, M., August, D., & Snow, C. E. (2005). Sustained vocabulary-learning strategies for English language learners. In E. H. Hiebert & M. Kamil (Eds.), *Teaching and learning vocabulary: Bringing research to practice* (pp. 137-153). Mahwah, NJ: Erlbaum.

Common Core State Standards Initiative. (2010). Common Core State Standards for English language arts and literacy in history/social studies, science, and technical subjects. Washington, DC: National Governors Association Center for Best Practices and the Council of Chief State School Officers.

Dressler, C., & Kamil, M. (2006). First- and second-language literacy. In D. August & TY. Shanahan (Eds.), Developing literacy in second-language learners: Report of the National Liteacy Panel on language minority children and youth (pp. 197-238). Mahwah, NJ: Erlbaum.

Fountas, I. & Pinnell, G. S. (2001). *Guiding readers and writers grades 3-6: Teaching comprehension, genre, and content literacy.*

NH: Heinemann.

Genesee, F., Geva, E., Dressler, D., & Kamil, M. (2006) Synthesis Cross linguistic relationships. In D. August & T. Shanahan (Eds.), *Developing literacy in second-language learners: Report of the National Literacy Panel on Language-Minority Children and Youth* (pp. 523-553). Mahwah, NJ: Erlbaum.

Goldenberg, C. (2008, summer). Teaching English language learners: What the research does and does not say. *American Educator*, 32(2), 8-44.

Goldenberg, C., & Coleman, R. (2010). *Promoting academic achievement among English language learners: A guide to the research*. Thousand Oaks, CA: Corwin.

Graves, M. F. (2006) *The vocabulary book: Learning and instruction*. New York: Teachers College Press.

Graves, M. F. (2009a). *Teaching individual words: One size does not fit all*. New York: Teachers College Press and International Reading Association.

Graves, M. F. Sales, F. C., & Ruda, M. A. (2012). *Word learning strategies*. Minneapolis: Seward, Inc.

Heimlich, J. E., & Pittelman, S. (1986). *Semantic mapping: Classroom applications*. Newark, DE: International Reading Association.

Johnson, D. D., & Pearson, P. D. (1978). *Teaching reading vocabulary*. New York: Holt, Rinehart & Winston.

Kame'enui, E. J., Carnine, D. W., Dixon, R. C., Simmons, D. C., & Coyne, M. D. (2002). *Effective teaching strategies that accommodate diverse learners*. OH: Prentice Hall.

Kieffer, M., & Lesaux, N. (2008). The role of derivational morphology in the reading comprehension of Spanish-speaking English language learners. *Reading and Writing*, 22, 993-1019.

Kuhn, M. R., & Stahl, S. A. (1998). Teaching children to learn word meanings from context: A synthesis and some questions. *Journal of Literacy Research*, 30, 119-138.

Lesaux, N., Kieffer, M., Faller, S. Ed., & Kelley, J. (2010). The effectiveness and ease of implementation of an academic vocabulary intervention for linguistically diverse students in urban middle schools. *Reading Research Quarterly*, 45, 196-228.

Marshall J. C. (2000). *Are they really reading?* ME: Stenhouse.

Marzano, R. J. (2004). *Building background knowledge for academic achievement*. Alexandria, VA: Association for Supervision and Curriculum Development.

McKeown, M. G., Beck, I. L., Omanson, R. C., & Pople, M. T. (1985). Some effects of the nature and frequency of vocabulary instruction on the knowledge and use of words. *Reading Research Quarterly*, 20, 522-535.

Miller, G. A., & Gildea, P. M. (1987). How children learn words. *Scientific American*, 257(3), 90-100.

Morrow, L. M., Gambrell, L., & Pressley, M. (2003). *Best practices in literacy instruction*. New York: Guilford.

Nagy, W. E. (2005). Why vocabulary instruction needs to be long-term and comprehensive. In E. Hiebert & M. Kamil (Eds.), *Teaching and learning vocabulary* (pp. 27-44). Mahwah, NJ:

Erlbaum.

Nagy, W. E. (2007). Metalinguistic awareness and the vocabulary-comprehension connection. In R. K. Wagner, A. Muse, & K. Tannenbaum (Eds.), *Vocabulary acquisition: Implications for reading comprehension* (pp. 52-77). New York: Guilford.

Nagy, W., Garcia, G., Durgunoglu, A., & Hancin-Bhatt, B. (1993). Spanish-English bilingual students' use of cognates in English Reading. Journal of Reading Behavior, 25, 241-259.

Nagy, W. E., & Scott, J. A. (2000). Vocabulary processes. In M. L. Kamil, P. B. Mosenthal, P. D. Pearson, & R. Barr (Eds.), Handbook of reading research (Vol. III, pp. 269-284) Mahwah, NJ: Erlbaum.

Nation, I. S. P. (2001). *Learning vocabulary in another language*. Cambridge, UK: Cambridge University Press.

Oller, D. K., & Eilers, R. E. (2002). *Language and literacy in bilingual children*. Clevedon, UK: Multilingual Matters.

Paribakht, T., & Wesche, M. (1999). Reading and "incidental" L2 vocabulary acquisition. *Studies in Second Language Acquisition*, 21, 195-224.

Pinker, S. (2000). *The language instinct: How the mind creates language*. New York: Harper-Perennial.

Pittelman, S. D., Heimlich, J. E., Berglund, R. L., & French, M. P. (1991). *Semantic feature analysis: Classroom applications*. Newark, DE: International Reading Association.

Routman, R. (2003). *Reading essentials: The specifics you need to teach reading well*. NH: Heinemann.

Samway, K., & Taylor, D. (2008). *Teaching English language learners*. New York: Scholastic.

Saville-Troike, M. (1984). What really matters in second language learning for academic achievement? *TESOL Quarterly*, 18(2), 199-219.

Schmitt, N. (2000). *Vocabulary in language teaching*. Cambridge, UK: Cambridge University Press.

Scott, J. A., & Nagy, W. E. (2004). Developing word consciousness. In J. F. Baumann & E. J. Kam'enui (Eds.), *Vocabulary instruction: Research to practice* (pp. 201-217). New York: Guildford Press.

Snow, C., & Kim, Y. (2007). Large problem spaces: The challenge of vocabulary for English language learners. In R. Wagner, A. Muse, & K. Tannenbaum (Eds.), *Vocabulary acquisition: Implications for reading comprehension* (pp. 123-136). New York: Guildford Press.

Stahl, S. A., & Nagy, W. E. (2006). *Teaching word meanings*. Mahwah, NJ: Erlbaum.

Sternberg, R. J. (1987). Most vocabulary is learned from context. In M. G. McKeown & M. E. Curtis (Eds.), *The nature of vocabulary acquisition* (pp. 89-105). Hillsdale, NJ: Erlbaum.

Swain, M. (2005) The output hypothesis: Theory an research. In Hinkel, E. (Eds.), *Handbook of research in second language teaching and learning* (pp. 471-483). Mahwah, NJ: Erlbaum.

Swanborn, M., & de Glopper, K. (1999). Incidental word learning while reading: A meta-analysis. *Review of Educational Research*, 69, 261-285.

Tovani, C. (2000). *I read it, but I don't get it: Comprehension strategies for adolescent readers*. ME: Stenhouse.

Trelease, J. (2006). *The read-aloud handbook* (6th ed.). New York: Penguin.

Ulanoff, S. H., & Pucci, S. L. (1999). Learning words from books: The effect of read aloud on second language vocabulary acquisition. *Bilingual Research Journal*, 23(4), 409-422.

White, T. G., Power, M. A., & White, S. (1989). Morphological analysis: Implications for teaching and understanding vocabulary growth. *Reading Research Quarterly*, 24, 283-304.

White, T. G., Sowell, J., & Yanagihara, A. (1989). Teaching elementary students to use word-part clues. *The Reading Teacher*, 42, 302-308.

Xu, S. H. (2010). *Teaching English language learners: Literacy strategies and resources for k-6*. New York: Guilford.

www.ingramcontent.com/pod-product-compliance
Lightning Source LLC
Chambersburg PA
CBHW071729090426
42738CB00011B/2432